THE MONEY EQUATION

How to Make More, Save More, and Live Richer

Dedication

To all seekers of financial empowerment,

This book is dedicated to you. May it be your compass, guiding you to make more, save more, and live richer.

Contents

Introduction

In the vast landscape of personal finance, there exists a powerful equation that can transform the way we interact with money, paving the way to a more prosperous and fulfilling life. Welcome to "The Money Equation: How to Make More, Save More, and Live Richer" – a comprehensive guide designed to unravel the mysteries of financial success and empower you to take control of your financial destiny.

A life lived with financial freedom is not just a dream; it is an achievable reality for anyone willing to embark on the journey of understanding and mastering the money equation. At its core, this equation is a dynamic interplay of various components, each contributing to the overall picture of your financial well-being. From income to investments, expenses to savings, retirement planning to debt management, and everything in between –

every piece plays a vital role in shaping your financial future.

Chapter by chapter, we will delve into the key elements that comprise the money equation, equipping you with the knowledge and tools needed to make informed financial decisions. This book is not just about quick fixes or overnight success; it is about cultivating a mindset and adopting practical strategies that build a strong foundation for lasting financial prosperity.

In "Chapter 1: Your Money Mindset," we lay the groundwork for success by exploring the pivotal role of mindset in financial achievement. We delve into the power of positive thinking and provide actionable steps to overcome any limiting beliefs that might be holding you back from your true potential.

Next, in "Chapter 2: Your Income," we uncover proven strategies to increase your earnings, whether through salary negotiations or identifying higher-paying job opportunities. But we don't stop there; we also dive into the world of passive income, offering insights into generating money even while you sleep.

In "Chapter 3: Your Expenses," we tackle the often-overlooked aspect of financial management: controlling your spending. By implementing practical techniques to track and reduce expenses, you can create a sustainable budget that aligns with your financial goals.

Saving money is a cornerstone of financial stability, and that's the focus of "Chapter 4: Your Savings." We emphasize the importance of saving regularly and set realistic goals that foster a healthy financial future. Moreover, we introduce the concept of automating savings, making it effortless and consistent.

Once you have a solid savings foundation, "Chapter 5: Your Investments" is your gateway to wealth accumulation. Whether you are a seasoned investor or just starting, we demystify the various investment options and guide you in making choices that align with your risk tolerance and objectives.

As we look towards the future, "Chapter 6: Your Retirement Planning" takes center stage. Together, we calculate how much you need to retire comfortably and explore different retirement plans that help you secure your golden years.

Debt can be a significant barrier to financial freedom, which is why "Chapter 7: Your Debt Management" is devoted to understanding and tackling various types of debt efficiently. We provide strategies to reduce and manage debt while rebuilding your credit score.

Understanding and optimizing your tax strategy is vital for maximizing your financial potential. In "Chapter 8: Your Tax Strategy," we delve into the complex world of taxes, equipping you with knowledge that allows you to keep more of your hard-earned money.

No comprehensive financial plan is complete without addressing risk management. In "Chapter 9: Your Insurance Coverage," we explore the importance of insurance and how to choose policies that protect your assets and loved ones without breaking the bank.

Preserving and growing wealth for future generations is a responsibility that lies within "Chapter 10: Your Wealth Preservation & Financial Education." We discuss estate planning, charitable giving, and the significance of continuous financial education.

Finally, we arrive at the ultimate goal – financial freedom. In "Chapter 11: Your Financial Freedom," we define this milestone and outline the actionable steps to achieve it. By embracing the principles discussed throughout the book, you can enjoy the peace and empowerment that financial freedom brings.

This book is not a mere compilation of financial advice but a roadmap to personal transformation. Throughout your journey, we encourage you to take action, make decisions with intention, and maintain unwavering determination.

Are you ready to unlock the power of the money equation and forge a path towards a richer and more fulfilled life? Let us embark on this life-changing expedition together, as we unravel the secrets of financial success, one chapter at a time. Your journey to financial freedom begins now.

What is the Money Equation?

The Money Equation is a dynamic and multifaceted concept that serves as the guiding principle to attain financial prosperity and independence. At its core, it is a holistic approach that harmonizes various elements of personal finance to help you make more, save more, and ultimately live a richer life.

Think of the Money Equation as a balanced formula, where each component represents a critical aspect of your financial well-being. This equation is not rigid; instead, it adapts to your unique circumstances, goals, and values. By understanding and optimizing each element, you can create a solid financial foundation that empowers you to weather life's uncertainties and seize opportunities for growth.

Let's break down the key elements that constitute the Money Equation:

Your Money Mindset: The first building block is your mindset – the beliefs, attitudes, and perceptions you hold about money. A positive money mindset is essential for success, as it influences your financial decisions and behaviors. By cultivating a growth-oriented mindset and dismantling limiting beliefs, you can unlock the potential for greater financial achievements.

Your Income: Your earnings play a pivotal role in the Money Equation. Increasing your income through various means, such as salary negotiations, career advancements, or additional income streams, provides more resources to allocate towards savings and investments.

Your Expenses: Managing your expenses is equally crucial. Tracking and curbing unnecessary spending allows you to free up funds that can be channeled towards savings and investment goals.

Your Savings: Savings are the cornerstone of financial stability. By setting clear savings goals and automating your contributions, you ensure that you consistently allocate a portion of your income for the future.

Your Investments: Investing your savings wisely helps your wealth grow exponentially over time. Understanding different investment options and aligning them with your risk tolerance and financial objectives are integral components of the Money Equation.

Your Retirement Planning: Planning for retirement ensures that you can maintain your desired lifestyle even after you stop working. Assessing the amount needed for a comfortable retirement and selecting suitable retirement plans are critical considerations.

Your Debt Management: Reducing and managing debt is a critical step towards achieving financial freedom. Addressing various types of debt and devising effective repayment strategies contribute to overall financial well-being.

Your Tax Strategy: A well-thought-out tax strategy can significantly impact your financial situation. By understanding tax planning and making smart tax-efficient decisions, you can optimize your tax burden.

Your Insurance Coverage: Insurance provides protection against unforeseen events that could derail your financial progress. Adequate coverage ensures that you and your loved ones are shielded from potential financial hardships.

Your Wealth Preservation & Financial Education: Preserving and growing wealth requires continuous learning and proactive financial planning. Estate planning, charitable giving, and a commitment to ongoing financial education are vital components of this aspect.

By integrating these elements and taking a comprehensive approach to your finances, you empower yourself to achieve financial freedom – the ultimate goal of the Money Equation. Financial freedom allows you to make life choices without being overly constrained by financial constraints, providing you the freedom to pursue your passions, embrace opportunities, and live life on your terms.

Throughout this book, we will explore each facet of the Money Equation in depth, equipping you with the knowledge and tools needed to transform your financial reality. The journey to financial empowerment starts now as we embark on this transformative quest together. So, let's take that first step and uncover the true potential of the Money

Equation – your path to making more, saving more, and living a richer life.

Importance of Understanding the Money Equation

The significance of comprehending the Money Equation cannot be overstated. It is not merely a set of abstract principles but a practical roadmap that empowers you to take control of your financial destiny. Understanding the Money Equation opens the door to a multitude of benefits that can significantly impact your life:

Financial Clarity and Confidence: When you grasp the various elements of the Money Equation, you gain a clear understanding of your financial situation. This clarity allows you to make informed decisions with confidence, enabling you to navigate financial challenges with ease.

Goal Setting and Achievement: The Money Equation provides a structured approach to setting and achieving financial goals. Whether it's saving for a dream vacation, purchasing a home, or planning for retirement, you can establish realistic objectives and create actionable plans to reach them.

Improved Financial Well-Being: By optimizing each component of the Money Equation, you create a balanced and resilient financial foundation. A positive money mindset, combined with strategic income growth, expense management, savings, and investments, contributes to enhanced overall financial well-being.

Enhanced Financial Security: Through prudent debt management, adequate insurance coverage, and tax-efficient strategies, you build a safety net that shields you from unexpected financial setbacks. This security provides peace of mind for you and your loved ones.

Wealth Accumulation and Growth: The Money Equation unlocks the potential for wealth accumulation and growth. By making intelligent investment choices and preserving your wealth effectively, you position yourself to achieve long-term financial prosperity.

Retirement Readiness: Planning for retirement is essential to ensure a comfortable and worry-free future. Understanding the Money Equation helps you navigate the complexities of retirement planning, assuring that you are adequately prepared for your golden years.

Financial Independence: The ultimate goal of the Money Equation is to attain financial freedom. This freedom liberates you from financial constraints, enabling you to pursue your passions, explore new opportunities, and live life on your terms.

Reduced Stress and Anxiety: Financial stress can be a significant burden on mental health. By embracing the principles of the Money Equation, you can alleviate financial worries and focus on leading a fulfilling and purpose-driven life.

Empowerment and Self-Reliance: A comprehensive understanding of the Money Equation empowers you to take control of your financial future. Instead of relying on luck or external factors, you become self-reliant in navigating your financial journey.

Legacy and Generational Impact: By implementing effective wealth preservation strategies, you can leave a lasting legacy for future generations. Charitable giving and responsible estate planning allow you to impact not only your life but also the lives of those you care about.

In this book, we delve deep into each component of the Money Equation, providing you with practical insights, actionable steps, and real-life examples to illustrate its transformative power. By absorbing and implementing the wisdom shared in these pages, you embark on a path of financial empowerment and unlock the doors to a richer and more fulfilling life.

Are you ready to embrace the importance of understanding the Money Equation? Let us embark on this journey together as we equip you with the knowledge and tools to master your finances, achieve your dreams, and ultimately live a life of abundance and prosperity. The path to financial freedom begins here, and the possibilities are limitless. Let's make the most of this incredible opportunity and seize the keys to your financial success.

Benefits of Financial Understanding

Financial understanding is more than just a skill; it is a transformative mindset that has far-reaching benefits across all aspects of your life. As you embark on the journey of comprehending and mastering your finances, you unlock a wealth of advantages that can profoundly impact your present and future. Let us explore the numerous benefits that come with financial understanding:

Empowerment and Control: Knowledge is power, and financial understanding empowers you to take full control of your financial life. When you possess the know-how to manage your money wisely, you can confidently make informed decisions, ensuring that your financial choices align with your aspirations and values.

Confidence in Decision-Making: Understanding your finances instills a sense of confidence in your ability to navigate complex financial situations. Whether it's investing in the stock market, negotiating a mortgage, or choosing the right insurance policy, your newfound understanding empowers you to make decisions that positively impact your financial future.

Improved Money Management: Financial understanding equips you with the tools to manage your money effectively. You can track your income and expenses, create budgets, and allocate resources strategically, allowing you to optimize your financial resources and avoid unnecessary debt.

Reduced Stress and Anxiety: Financial stress is a common source of anxiety for many individuals. By developing financial literacy, you gain the ability to plan for the future, build emergency funds, and safeguard against unexpected events. As a result, you can enjoy greater peace of mind and reduced anxiety about financial uncertainties.

Goal Achievement and Aspirations: Armed with financial understanding, you can set clear financial goals and craft actionable plans to achieve them. Whether your aspirations involve buying a home, traveling the world, or retiring early, your financial acumen paves the way to transform dreams into reality.

Building Wealth and Security: Financial literacy is a steppingstone to building and preserving wealth. You can implement sound investment strategies, optimize tax planning, and manage debt responsibly, all contributing to long-term financial security and prosperity.

Economic Resilience: In times of economic turbulence, financial understanding acts as a shield against financial hardships. With a well-prepared financial plan, you can weather economic downturns and emerge stronger on the other side.

Enhanced Family Well-Being: A deep understanding of finances benefits not only you but also your family. By making informed financial decisions, you can ensure the well-being and future security of your loved ones, fostering a stable and nurturing environment.

Generational Impact: Financial literacy has the power to create a positive ripple effect that extends to future generations. By passing on your knowledge and values surrounding money, you can empower your children and grandchildren to make sound financial choices, leaving a lasting legacy of financial well-being.

Freedom and Flexibility: Financial understanding grants you the freedom to explore life's opportunities without being shackled by financial constraints. Whether it's pursuing your dream career, starting a business, or taking sabbaticals for personal growth, your financial prowess provides the flexibility to embrace life on your terms.

Contributing to the Community: When you possess financial understanding, you are better equipped to give back to your community and support charitable causes. Your financial stability allows you to make a positive impact on the lives of others and contribute to meaningful social change.

A Path to Financial Freedom: Ultimately, financial understanding is the key to unlocking the door to financial freedom. It grants you the ability to achieve your desired level of financial independence, allowing you to live life fully and pursue your passions without being held captive by financial worries.

In this book, we aim to impart the knowledge and insights that empower you to reap these numerous benefits. Through a comprehensive exploration of the Money Equation, we equip you with practical tools, real-life examples, and actionable strategies that transform your financial reality.

Are you ready to seize the countless advantages that come with financial understanding? Join us on this transformative journey as we unlock the door to a richer and more fulfilling life. Let us walk hand in hand towards a brighter financial future where your dreams become your reality, and financial freedom becomes your everyday truth. Embrace the power of financial understanding and prepare to embark on a life-changing expedition. The path to financial prosperity starts here.

Chapter 1: Your Money Mindset

Your mindset is a potent force that shapes your financial journey. This chapter highlights the influence of your thoughts and beliefs about money on your overall financial success. By developing a positive money mindset and addressing negative beliefs, you can unlock your full potential to make more, save more, and live a richer life.

• *The Role of Mindset in Financial Success*

Your mindset is the foundation upon which your financial success is built. It is the way you perceive and approach money, wealth, and financial decisions. A positive and empowering money mindset can be a catalyst for achieving your financial goals, while a negative mindset can hold you back and hinder your progress. Understanding the role of mindset in financial success is crucial in transforming your relationship with money and creating a path to a richer life.

The Power of Beliefs: Your beliefs about money shape your financial reality. If you hold limiting beliefs such as "money is the root of all evil" or "I will never be wealthy," these beliefs can become self-fulfilling prophecies. Recognizing and challenging these limiting beliefs is essential for fostering a mindset that supports abundance and growth.

Cultivating a Growth Mindset: Embracing a growth mindset means seeing challenges as opportunities for learning and improvement. Financial success often involves taking risks and stepping out of your comfort zone. With a growth mindset, you can approach financial challenges with resilience and adaptability, leading to greater financial rewards.

Goal Setting and Visualization: Visualizing your financial goals and imagining yourself achieving them can have a powerful impact on your actions and decisions. By vividly seeing yourself reaching your financial milestones, you create a stronger sense of purpose and motivation, driving you forward in your financial journey.

Developing Financial Confidence: Confidence in your ability to manage money and make sound financial choices is vital for success. Building financial confidence involves educating yourself about personal finance, seeking advice from experts, and taking small steps towards financial empowerment.

Gratitude and Abundance: Cultivating an attitude of gratitude for what you have and embracing a mindset of abundance can shift your focus from scarcity to opportunities. Acknowledging the resources and opportunities available to you opens up new possibilities for wealth creation.

Mindfulness in Spending: Mindless spending can lead to financial leaks and hinder your ability to save and invest. Practicing mindfulness in your financial decisions allows you to align your spending with your values and long-term goals, ultimately contributing to financial well-being.

Surrounding Yourself with Positivity: The people you surround yourself with can influence your mindset. Surrounding yourself with positive and financially-minded individuals can inspire and encourage you on your financial journey.

In this chapter, we will explore the power of mindset in financial success and provide practical strategies to develop a positive money mindset. By understanding the influence of your thoughts and beliefs on your financial outcomes, you can lay a solid foundation for making more, saving more, and living a richer life. Let us embark on this transformative journey to unlock the true potential of your money equation.

• *Developing a Positive Money Mindset*

Developing a positive money mindset is a transformative process that empowers you to see money as a tool for growth, abundance, and achieving your financial goals. By nurturing a positive relationship with money, you can overcome limiting beliefs, build financial confidence, and attract opportunities for wealth creation. This chapter will guide you through practical steps to cultivate a positive money mindset and unlock your full potential on the path to financial success.

Self-Awareness and Reflection: The journey to a positive money mindset begins with self-awareness. Take the time to reflect on your beliefs and attitudes towards money. Identify any negative patterns or self-limiting thoughts that may be holding you back from financial abundance. Understanding your money story allows you to consciously rewrite it into a narrative that supports your financial growth.

Affirmations and Positive Declarations: Affirmations are powerful tools for reshaping your subconscious mind. Create positive affirmations that reinforce your financial goals and aspirations. Repeat these affirmations daily, preferably in front of a mirror, to instill them deeply into your psyche. Affirmations such as "I attract abundance and prosperity" and "I am worthy of financial success" can reprogram your mind for positive financial outcomes.

Gratitude Practice: Gratitude is a key component of a positive money mindset. Regularly express gratitude for the money you have, the opportunities before you, and the progress you've made on your financial journey. A gratitude journal can be a valuable tool for recording the things you are grateful for related to money and finance, helping you maintain a positive perspective.

Embrace Mistakes and Failures: Adopting a positive money mindset means viewing mistakes and failures as valuable learning experiences rather than setbacks. Embrace these moments as opportunities to grow and refine your financial decision-making. Remember, even the most successful individuals faced challenges on their path to financial prosperity.

Focus on Abundance, Not Scarcity: Shift your focus from scarcity to abundance. Instead of dwelling on what you lack, focus on the resources and opportunities available to you. Cultivate an abundance mindset by celebrating your financial wins, no matter how small, and acknowledging the potential for more abundance in your life.

Set Realistic Financial Goals: Break down your long-term financial goals into smaller, achievable milestones. Celebrate each milestone as you reach them, reinforcing your belief in your ability to achieve bigger goals. Setting realistic and attainable financial goals promotes a positive outlook on your financial future.

Surround Yourself with Positivity: Your environment significantly impacts your mindset. Surround yourself with people who uplift and inspire you on your financial journey. Engage with positive financial content, books, podcasts, or seminars that reinforce a healthy money mindset.

Practice Gratitude-Based Spending: Before making purchases, consider whether the expense aligns with your values and priorities. Engage in gratitude-based spending, where you spend money on things that genuinely bring joy and fulfillment, rather than seeking temporary gratification from impulse purchases.

Visualize Financial Success: Visualization is a powerful tool for manifesting your financial desires. Regularly visualize yourself achieving your financial goals, experiencing the emotions of success, and living a life of financial abundance. Allow these visualizations to create a sense of certainty and confidence in your financial journey.

Seek Support and Education: Developing a positive money mindset is an ongoing process, and seeking support and education can accelerate your progress. Attend workshops, read books, or participate in online forums that focus on personal finance and mindset development.

By diligently practicing these strategies, you can transform your relationship with money and develop a resilient, positive money mindset. Remember, every small shift in mindset contributes to your overall financial well-being. With this newfound mindset, you are ready to tackle the rest of the money equation and embark on a journey towards making more, saving more, and living a richer life.

• *Overcoming Negative Money Beliefs*

Negative money beliefs can act as significant barriers to financial success and well-being. These beliefs often stem from past experiences, upbringing, and societal conditioning. However, by identifying and addressing these limiting beliefs, you can reshape your money mindset and open the door to new financial possibilities. In this chapter, we will explore effective strategies to overcome negative money beliefs and replace them with empowering perspectives that support your journey to financial abundance.

Recognize and Challenge Limiting Beliefs: The first step in overcoming negative money beliefs is to become aware of them. Take some time for self-reflection to identify any recurring negative thoughts or beliefs you hold about money. These may include beliefs such as "money is the root of all evil" or "I will never be good with money." Challenge these beliefs by asking yourself if they are based on facts or simply inherited assumptions.

Understand the Origin of Your Beliefs: Negative money beliefs often have deep roots in our past experiences and upbringing. Reflect on how your family's attitudes towards money and wealth may have influenced your current beliefs. Understanding the origin of your beliefs can help you separate them from your true financial potential.

Reframe Negative Thoughts: Once you've identified negative money beliefs, work on reframing them into more positive and empowering statements. For example, change "I will never be good with money" to "I am capable of learning and improving my financial skills." Practice these reframed statements regularly to reinforce a positive money mindset.

Surround Yourself with Positive Influences: Seek out individuals who have a healthy and positive attitude towards money. Engage with mentors, friends, or financial experts who can provide encouragement and support in challenging your negative beliefs. Positive influences can inspire you to adopt more constructive beliefs and behaviors.

Practice Gratitude for Financial Growth: Cultivate gratitude for your financial progress, no matter how small it may seem. Celebrate each step forward and acknowledge your efforts in improving your financial situation. Focusing on what you have achieved rather than what you lack can shift your perspective towards abundance.

Set Realistic Financial Goals: Setting achievable financial goals and accomplishing them can boost your confidence and prove to yourself that you can overcome challenges. By achieving these milestones, you challenge negative beliefs and create evidence of your financial capabilities.

Seek Professional Guidance: If certain negative money beliefs persist, consider seeking guidance from a financial counselor, therapist, or coach. These professionals can help you explore the underlying causes of your beliefs and provide tailored strategies to address them effectively.

Practice Mindfulness: Be mindful of your thoughts and emotions related to money. When negative beliefs arise, acknowledge them without judgment, and consciously choose to replace them with more positive affirmations. Mindfulness helps you become more aware of the patterns of thought that influence your financial decisions.

Embrace a Growth Mindset: Adopt a growth mindset in your financial journey. Recognize that your current financial situation does not define your future potential. Embrace challenges as opportunities for growth and learning, and believe in your ability to develop new financial skills and habits.

Focus on Personal Progress: Avoid comparing your financial situation with others, as this can reinforce negative beliefs. Instead, focus on your personal progress and celebrate the unique steps you take towards financial improvement.

By implementing these strategies consistently, you can gradually dismantle negative money beliefs and replace them with positive, empowering beliefs. Overcoming these limiting beliefs is a crucial step towards developing a positive money mindset and creating the foundation for lasting financial success. As you continue your financial journey, remember that your thoughts and beliefs have a significant impact on your actions and outcomes. Embrace the power of positivity and let it guide you toward making more, saving more, and living a richer life.

Chapter 2: Your Income

Learn how to increase your earnings with proven strategies for financial growth and stability. Discover ways to maximize your current job's potential and explore new opportunities to achieve financial independence and prosperity.

• *Strategies to Increase Your Income*

A. Evaluate Your Current Skills and Expertise.

To increase your income, start by assessing your existing skills and expertise. Identify areas where you excel and explore how you can leverage these strengths to pursue higher-paying opportunities. Consider whether there are specialized certifications, additional education, or training that could enhance your skill set and make you more valuable in the job market.

B. Pursue Professional Development.

Continuing education and professional development are essential for staying relevant in today's ever-changing job landscape. Invest in courses, workshops, or seminars that align with your career goals and can lead to promotions or salary increases. Not only will this enhance your skills, but it will also demonstrate to employers or clients that you are committed to personal growth and self-improvement.

C. Seek Career Advancement Opportunities.

Advancing in your current job or seeking better career opportunities elsewhere can significantly impact your income. Talk to your supervisors about your career aspirations and ask for feedback on how to progress within the company. Be proactive in seeking out promotions or lateral moves that can lead to higher salaries and better benefits.

D. Leverage Negotiation Skills.

Negotiating your salary during job interviews or performance reviews is a crucial skill for increasing your income. Research salary benchmarks for your position and industry to ensure you are advocating for fair compensation. Highlight your achievements, the value you bring to the organization, and any additional responsibilities you have taken on to strengthen your negotiation position.

E. Explore Side Hustles or Freelancing.

Consider starting a side business or freelancing in your spare time to supplement your primary income. Side hustles allow you to explore your passions, diversify your income streams, and potentially grow into profitable ventures. It's essential to find a side hustle that aligns with your skills and interests, ensuring that it remains manageable and enjoyable.

F. Invest in Passive Income Streams.

Passive income streams can provide a steady flow of money without requiring constant active effort. Look into various passive income opportunities, such as investing in dividend-paying stocks, rental properties, or peer-to-peer lending platforms. While building passive income may take time and effort initially, it can lead to long-term financial stability and increased earnings.

G. Network and Build Professional Relationships.

Networking is a powerful tool for uncovering new job opportunities and career advancements. Attend industry events, join professional associations, and engage with like-minded individuals in your field. Building a strong network can lead to referrals, job offers, or potential collaborations that might not be advertised publicly.

H. Embrace Entrepreneurship.

For those with an entrepreneurial spirit, starting a business can be a rewarding way to increase income. Identify gaps in the market or explore innovative solutions to existing problems. Building a successful business can lead to significant financial rewards, but it's essential to conduct thorough market research and create a solid business plan before taking the plunge.

I. Stay Agile and Adapt to Changing Market Trends.

The job market is dynamic, with new opportunities emerging while others become less in demand. Stay agile and continuously assess industry trends and technological advancements that could affect your career path. Be willing to adapt your skills and expertise to stay relevant and seize opportunities for career growth and income enhancement.

J. Consider Remote Work or Freelancing Platforms.

Remote work and freelancing platforms offer opportunities to work with clients from around the world and access a broader range of projects and gigs. Embracing remote work or utilizing freelancing platforms can provide access to higher-paying assignments and clients with diverse needs, expanding your earning potential.

Remember, increasing your income requires a combination of ambition, proactive effort, and a willingness to invest in your professional development. By implementing these strategies, you can take significant steps toward achieving financial growth and living a richer life.

• *Negotiating Your Salary Effectively*

Negotiating your salary is a critical skill that can significantly impact your income and financial well-being. Many people feel uncomfortable discussing money matters, but with proper preparation and confidence, you can successfully negotiate a salary that reflects your true value. Here are essential tips to help you negotiate your salary effectively:

Research Salary Benchmarks:

Before entering into a salary negotiation, research industry salary benchmarks for your position and location. Websites like Glassdoor, Payscale, and LinkedIn Salary Insights can provide valuable data on average salaries for similar roles. This information will give you a realistic range to aim for during negotiations.

Highlight Your Achievements:

During the negotiation, emphasize your accomplishments and the value you have brought to your current or previous roles. Discuss specific projects you've excelled in, your contributions to team success, and any unique skills that set you apart. Demonstrating your worth can reinforce the idea that you deserve a higher salary.

Know Your Market Value:

Understand the demand for your skills and experience in the job market. If your profession is in high demand, you have more negotiating power. Research industry trends and job openings to gauge how sought-after your expertise is, which can be used as leverage during the negotiation.

Practice Effective Communication:

Confidence and clarity are essential when negotiating your salary. Practice your pitch beforehand, focusing on concise and persuasive communication. Avoid vague language and be specific about the salary you desire. Be prepared to explain why you believe you deserve the proposed increase.

Timing Matters:

Timing plays a crucial role in salary negotiations. The best time to discuss salary is during the final stages of the job interview process when the employer has already shown interest in hiring you. If you're already employed, consider requesting a salary review during performance evaluations or when you've accomplished significant milestones for the company.

Be Open to Other Perks:

Salary negotiations aren't solely about base pay. Consider other benefits and perks that may be negotiable, such as bonuses, stock options, flexible working hours, or additional vacation days. If the employer is unable to meet your desired salary, they might be more willing to enhance other aspects of the compensation package.

Stay Professional and Positive:

Approach salary negotiations with a positive attitude and professionalism. Avoid ultimatums or threats, as they can damage your reputation and hinder future career opportunities. Instead, focus on building a collaborative relationship with your employer while advocating for your worth.

Practice Active Listening:

Listening is as important as speaking during negotiations. Pay attention to what the employer is saying and be open to understanding their perspective. Address their concerns or objections with thoughtful responses, showing that you're willing to find a mutually beneficial solution.

Consider Long-Term Growth:

While negotiating for a higher salary, think about the potential for growth and development within the company. Discuss opportunities for career advancement, additional responsibilities, or professional development programs. Demonstrating your commitment to your long-term success can be advantageous during negotiations.

Be Prepared to Walk Away:

Negotiating a salary increase may not always yield the desired outcome. Be prepared to walk away if the offer does not meet your expectations and align with your value. Sometimes, declining an inadequate offer can lead to better opportunities in the future.

Remember, negotiating your salary is a normal and expected part of the hiring process or annual performance review. By being well-prepared, confident, and professional, you can increase your chances of securing a salary that reflects your true worth and contributes to your overall financial success.

• *Exploring Opportunities for Higher-Paying Jobs*

Exploring opportunities for higher-paying jobs is a proactive approach to increasing your income and achieving your financial goals. While advancing within your current company is one way to boost your earnings, it's essential to keep your options open and consider external opportunities that align with your skills and ambitions. Here are effective strategies to explore higher-paying jobs:

Update Your Resume and LinkedIn Profile:

Before embarking on your job search, ensure that your resume and LinkedIn profile are up-to-date and showcase your skills, experiences, and achievements. Tailor your resume to highlight the qualifications that make you an attractive candidate for higher-paying roles.

Leverage Your Network:

Your professional network can be a valuable resource when seeking higher-paying jobs. Inform your connections about your job search and express your career aspirations. Attend networking events, industry conferences, and webinars to expand your network and gain insights into potential job opportunities.

Utilize Online Job Platforms:

Explore job search websites and platforms that cater to your industry or profession. Websites like Indeed, LinkedIn Job Search, and industry-specific job boards often feature a wide range of job openings, including higher-paying positions.

Reach Out to Recruitment Agencies:

Recruitment agencies specialize in matching candidates with suitable job opportunities. Consider registering with reputable agencies in your field, as they may have access to exclusive job openings with competitive salaries.

Attend Career Fairs:

Career fairs provide an excellent opportunity to meet employers face-to-face and learn about available job positions. Dress professionally, bring copies of your resume, and prepare to engage with potential employers.

Research Companies Known for Competitive Salaries:

Conduct research to identify companies that are known for offering higher salaries and excellent employee benefits. Look for organizations that prioritize employee satisfaction, career growth, and work-life balance.

Consider Relocation:

Higher-paying job opportunities may not always be available in your current location. Be open to the possibility of relocation if it aligns with your career goals and improves your overall compensation package.

Develop In-Demand Skills:

Identify skills that are in high demand within your industry and invest time in developing them. Acquiring sought-after skills can make you a more valuable candidate, potentially leading to higher-paying job offers.

Seek Mentorship and Career Guidance:

Mentors and career coaches can offer valuable guidance in your job search and help you strategize for career growth. Their insights and advice can assist you in making informed decisions to secure higher-paying roles.

Stay Persistent and Patient:

Finding a higher-paying job may take time and persistence. Stay committed to your job search efforts and maintain a positive attitude even in the face of rejection. Remember that finding the right opportunity is a process that requires patience.

Prepare for Interviews:

Be well-prepared for job interviews by researching the company, understanding its values and culture, and rehearsing your responses to common interview questions. Show enthusiasm for the position and demonstrate how your skills align with the company's needs.

Negotiate Your Salary:

Once you receive a job offer, don't hesitate to negotiate your salary. Use the research you conducted on industry salary benchmarks to advocate for fair compensation that reflects your skills and experience.

Exploring opportunities for higher-paying jobs is a proactive step towards achieving financial growth and professional fulfillment. By leveraging your network, utilizing online resources, and continuously improving your skills, you can increase your chances of finding a rewarding career with the compensation you deserve. Remember to be persistent, patient, and confident throughout your job search journey.

Chapter 3: Your Expenses

Discover the foundation of sound financial management by understanding the significance of tracking your expenses. Uncover how seemingly minor spending decisions can have a substantial impact on your overall financial health. This chapter equips you with invaluable techniques and tools to gain control over your finances, empowering you to make informed decisions and pursue a richer future.

• *Importance of Tracking Expenses*

In the pursuit of financial well-being and living richer, tracking expenses emerges as a fundamental pillar of sound money management. The chapter on Your Expenses delves into the vital importance of monitoring and understanding your spending habits. Tracking expenses serves as a crucial tool that empowers individuals to take control of their financial lives and make informed decisions. Here's why it is essential:

Increased Financial Awareness: When you track your expenses, you gain a clear and accurate picture of where your money is going. It allows you to identify patterns, recognize spending leaks, and understand areas where you can potentially cut back. By being aware of your financial behaviors, you can make conscious choices about how you allocate your resources.

Budgeting Precision: An accurate expense tracking system is the cornerstone of an effective budget. By analyzing your spending history, you can create a realistic and achievable budget that aligns with your financial goals. Budgeting helps you prioritize essential expenses, allocate funds to savings, investments, and debt repayment, and avoid unnecessary splurges.

Identifying Financial Habits: Tracking expenses provides insights into your financial habits and tendencies. It enables you to distinguish between needs and wants and fosters a more mindful approach to spending. Understanding your habits allows you to take corrective actions and establish healthier financial practices.

Empowering Decision Making: Armed with knowledge about your spending patterns, you can make informed decisions about how to optimize your financial resources. Whether it's deciding on major purchases, evaluating subscription services, or comparing different utility providers, tracking expenses empowers you to choose options that align with your financial priorities.

Debt Reduction and Financial Goals: For those striving to pay off debts or achieve specific financial objectives, tracking expenses is a powerful tool. By identifying areas to cut costs or free up additional funds, you can accelerate debt repayment and make progress toward your goals faster.

Motivation for Change: As you observe your financial progress over time, tracking expenses can be highly motivating. Witnessing improvements in your spending habits and seeing the impact of your efforts can encourage you to stay on course and continue making positive changes.

Enhanced Financial Stability: Tracking expenses contributes to greater financial stability. With a better grasp of your cash flow, you can manage unexpected expenses more effectively and build an emergency fund to weather challenging times without jeopardizing your long-term financial plans.

Building a Strong Financial Foundation: Consistent expense tracking lays the groundwork for long-term financial success. It instills discipline and responsibility, promoting a more responsible and thoughtful approach to handling money.

Tracking expenses is not just an administrative task; it is a powerful tool for transforming your financial life. By monitoring your spending, you gain a deep understanding of your financial habits, enabling you to budget wisely, reduce debt, and achieve your financial aspirations. Embracing the practice of tracking expenses is a crucial step towards mastering the money equation and ultimately living a richer and more fulfilling life.

• *Techniques for Cutting Unnecessary Expenses*

Managing your expenses effectively is a key component of achieving financial success. As you progress on your journey to make more, save more, and live richer, adopting techniques to cut unnecessary expenses becomes vital in optimizing your financial resources. This chapter explores practical and actionable strategies that will help you identify and trim wasteful spending, empowering you to take charge of your financial future.

Conduct a Comprehensive Expense Audit:

Begin by conducting a thorough expense audit. Review your bank statements, credit card bills, and receipts to categorize your spending. This exercise will shed light on areas where you are overspending and uncover expenses that can be reduced or eliminated.

Differentiate Between Needs and Wants:

Distinguish between essential needs and discretionary wants. Prioritize spending on necessities such as housing, utilities, groceries, and healthcare. Evaluate non-essential expenses, such as entertainment, dining out, or luxury purchases, and be prepared to cut back in these areas to free up funds for more critical financial goals.

Embrace Frugality:

Embracing a frugal mindset can significantly impact your spending habits. Seek cost-effective alternatives without sacrificing quality. Look for discounts, use coupons, and consider buying in bulk to save money on everyday purchases.

Minimize Impulse Buying:

Avoid impulsive purchases by creating a shopping list before heading to the store and sticking to it. If you find something you want but don't necessarily need, impose a cooling-off period before making the purchase. Often, you'll find that the desire to buy diminishes after some reflection.

Reduce Unnecessary Subscriptions:

Review your subscriptions and memberships regularly. Cancel those you no longer use or derive value from. Consider sharing subscriptions with family or friends to split costs or opt for free alternatives where possible.

Negotiate Bills and Contracts:

Don't be afraid to negotiate bills and contracts, such as internet, cable, or insurance. Research competitors' rates and approach your providers armed with information. Often, they may offer you better deals to retain your business.

Limit Eating Out and Cook at Home:

Eating out frequently can be a major drain on your finances. Limit dining out to special occasions and make cooking at home a regular practice. Not only will this save money, but it can also lead to healthier eating habits.

Reduce Transportation Costs:

Consider carpooling, using public transportation, or biking to work if feasible. These alternatives can significantly cut down on fuel and maintenance costs associated with daily commuting.

Avoid Unplanned ATM Withdrawals:

Plan your cash needs in advance to avoid unplanned ATM withdrawals that may incur additional fees. Stick to your budget and use your bank's ATM to minimize charges.

Track and Celebrate Progress:

Continuously monitor your spending and celebrate your achievements as you cut unnecessary expenses. Reward yourself for meeting financial goals, reinforcing positive behavior and making expense management an enjoyable process.

By implementing these techniques for cutting unnecessary expenses, you can create a stronger financial foundation, allocate more resources towards savings and investments, and accelerate your journey towards financial freedom. Embrace the power of conscious spending and take control of your financial destiny. Remember, every small saving counts, and together, they pave the way for a more prosperous future.

• *Creating a Practical and Effective Budget*

In the quest for financial stability and success, a well-crafted budget serves as a powerful roadmap to guide your financial decisions. Building and following a practical and effective budget is a cornerstone of the money equation, enabling you to align your income and expenses, achieve your financial goals, and live richer. This chapter outlines a step-by-step process for creating a budget that empowers you to take control of your finances with confidence.

Assess Your Financial Situation:

Begin by evaluating your current financial status. Calculate your total income from all sources, including salary, bonuses, side hustles, and investments. Next, list all your essential expenses, such as rent or mortgage, utilities, groceries, transportation, and debt payments. Understanding your financial baseline is crucial to building a realistic budget.

Categorize Your Expenses:

Divide your expenses into fixed and variable categories. Fixed expenses remain constant each month, while variable expenses fluctuate, often influenced by your discretionary choices. Categorization will help you identify areas where you have more control and can potentially reduce spending.

Set Specific Financial Goals:

Define clear and achievable financial goals. Whether you aim to pay off debts, save for a down payment on a house, or build an emergency fund, having specific objectives will give your budget a purpose and keep you motivated to stay on track.

Allocate Funds Wisely:

Prioritize your expenses based on necessity and importance. Allocate funds to essential needs first, such as housing, food, utilities, and debt repayment.

Once these essentials are covered, allocate money to savings, investments, and non-essential expenses in alignment with your financial goals.

Implement the 50/30/20 Rule:

A popular budgeting guideline is the 50/30/20 rule. Allocate 50% of your after-tax income to needs, 30% to wants or discretionary spending, and 20% to savings and debt repayment. This rule provides a balanced approach to budgeting, ensuring that you meet essential needs while still enjoying some flexibility in your discretionary spending.

Use Budgeting Tools:

Leverage technology to make budgeting easier and more efficient. Numerous budgeting apps and online tools are available to help you track expenses, set financial goals, and monitor progress in real-time.

Be Realistic and Flexible:

A successful budget should be realistic and flexible enough to accommodate unexpected expenses or changes in your financial situation. It's essential to be honest with yourself about your spending habits and make adjustments as needed to maintain a balanced budget.

Monitor and Review Regularly:

Creating a budget is only the first step; consistent monitoring and review are equally important. Regularly assess your progress, compare your actual spending to your budgeted amounts, and make adjustments as necessary. Stay proactive in managing your finances to ensure that you stay on course towards your financial goals.

Celebrate Milestones:

As you achieve milestones within your budget, take time to celebrate your successes. Recognizing your accomplishments will foster a positive attitude towards budgeting and reinforce your commitment to financial well-being.

By creating a practical and effective budget, you take charge of your financial destiny. Budgeting empowers you to make informed decisions, prioritize your financial goals, and live within your means while planning for a prosperous future. Embrace the power of budgeting as an essential tool in the money equation, guiding you towards financial freedom and the ability to live a richer and more fulfilling life.

Chapter 4: Your Savings

Savings are the foundation of financial stability and a gateway to realizing your dreams. In this chapter, we'll explore the importance of saving money and practical strategies to accelerate your savings journey. Whether you're building an emergency fund, saving for a home, or planning a dream vacation, understanding the power of saving and setting realistic goals are vital for securing your financial future. Let's uncover effective saving practices that will empower you to take control of your finances and live a richer life.

• *Understanding the Significance of Saving Money*

Saving money is a fundamental pillar of financial success and a crucial aspect of mastering the money equation. We will delve into the profound importance of saving and how it can profoundly impact your financial well-being both in the short term and long term.

Building Financial Security:

Saving money acts as a safety net, providing financial security in times of emergencies or unexpected events. Having an adequate savings cushion can shield you from the stress of unforeseen expenses, such as medical emergencies, car repairs, or job loss. We explore strategies to establish an emergency fund and how it can serve as a buffer against financial hardships.

Achieving Financial Goals:

Whether it's purchasing a home, going on a dream vacation, funding higher education, or starting a business, saving money is the key to making these aspirations a reality. We discuss the importance of setting specific savings goals and creating a plan to reach them efficiently. Learn how disciplined saving can turn dreams into achievable milestones.

Breaking the Debt Cycle:

Saving money not only helps you build wealth but also assists in breaking free from the burden of debt. By saving and accumulating funds, you can avoid relying on credit cards or loans for everyday expenses. We explore how strategic saving can accelerate debt repayment and empower you to regain control of your finances.

Harnessing the Power of Compound Interest:

One of the most significant advantages of saving is leveraging the power of compound interest. By letting your savings grow and earn interest over time, you can multiply your money exponentially. We unravel the concept of compound interest and how it can supercharge your savings for a more prosperous future.

Planning for Retirement:

Saving money plays a vital role in securing a comfortable retirement. In this section, we emphasize the significance of starting early and consistently contributing to retirement accounts. Learn about retirement planning options, such as employer-sponsored 401(k)s, IRAs (Individual Retirement Accounts), and other retirement vehicles, to ensure a financially stable post-working life.

Breaking the Paycheck-to-Paycheck Cycle:

Many individuals find themselves trapped in a paycheck-to-paycheck cycle, struggling to cover living expenses without any room for saving. We discuss practical steps to break free from this cycle, budget effectively, and allocate funds to savings to build a more secure financial future.

Preparing for Life's Uncertainties:

Life is full of uncertainties, such as job changes, economic fluctuations, and unexpected events. Saving money provides a safety net during uncertain times, allowing you to navigate through transitions with greater confidence and flexibility.

In this chapter, we uncover the profound significance of saving money and how it can be a transformative force in achieving financial stability, growth, and peace of mind. By understanding the true value of saving, you can take charge of your financial destiny and pave the way for a brighter, more prosperous future.

• *Setting Realistic Savings Goals*

Saving money is a powerful financial habit, but without clear and achievable goals, it can be challenging to stay motivated and on track. In this section, we'll explore the art of setting realistic savings goals that align with your financial aspirations and life circumstances.

Assessing Your Financial Situation:

Before diving into setting savings goals, it's essential to assess your current financial situation. Take a comprehensive look at your income, expenses, debts, and existing savings. Understanding where you stand financially will give you a realistic starting point for goal-setting.

Identifying Short-Term and Long-Term Goals:

Begin by distinguishing between short-term and long-term savings goals. Short-term goals may include creating an emergency fund, going on a vacation, or purchasing a new gadget. Long-term goals, on the other hand, might involve saving for a down payment on a home, funding your child's education, or building a substantial retirement nest egg.

Making Goals Specific and Measurable:

To make your savings goals more effective, make them specific and measurable. Define the exact amount you want to save and the timeframe in which you wish to achieve it. For instance, "Save $5,000 for an emergency fund within 12 months" is more actionable than a vague goal like "Save some money."

Creating a Realistic Timeline:

Be honest with yourself about how much you can save each month. Consider your income, expenses, and other financial obligations. While it's essential to challenge yourself, setting unattainable goals can lead to frustration and derail your saving efforts. Create a timeline that stretches you without causing undue financial strain.

Prioritizing Your Goals:

You may have multiple savings goals simultaneously, but it's crucial to prioritize them. Decide which goals are most important and focus your efforts on achieving them one by one. This approach allows you to allocate your resources effectively and achieve a sense of accomplishment as you reach each milestone.

Breaking Down Large Goals into Smaller Milestones:

If your long-term savings goals seem overwhelming, break them down into smaller, manageable milestones. Celebrate each milestone achieved and use it as motivation to keep moving forward.

Regularly Reviewing and Adjusting Your Goals:

Financial circumstances can change over time, so it's essential to review and adjust your savings goals periodically. Life events, unexpected expenses, or changes in income may require modifying your goals. Stay flexible and adapt your savings plan as needed to stay on track.

Leveraging Technology and Automation:

Take advantage of financial apps and tools that can help you monitor your progress and automate your savings. Automatic transfers to a dedicated savings account can ensure consistent progress toward your goals without requiring constant manual effort.

Seeking Professional Advice:

If you find goal-setting and financial planning overwhelming, don't hesitate to seek advice from a financial advisor. They can help you create a personalized savings strategy based on your unique circumstances and long-term objectives.

By setting realistic savings goals, you give yourself a roadmap to financial success. These goals will motivate and guide you as you embark on your journey to achieve greater financial security, freedom, and prosperity. Remember, every small step you take towards your savings goals brings you closer to living a richer and more fulfilling life.

- ## *Automating Your Savings for Consistency*

While setting savings goals is a critical step towards financial success, consistent execution is equally important. However, human nature can sometimes lead us astray, making it challenging to adhere to our saving objectives diligently. To address this, automating your savings can be a game-changing strategy to ensure regular contributions and stay on course. In this chapter, we explore the power of automating your savings and how it can revolutionize your financial journey.

The Psychology of Automation:

Automating your savings taps into the psychological principle of consistency and removes the temptation to spend money impulsively. By setting up automatic transfers, you establish a habit of saving, making it easier to stay committed to your financial goals over the long term.

Setting Up Automatic Transfers:

Most banks and financial institutions offer the option to set up recurring transfers between your checking and savings accounts. Choose a specific date each month, ideally aligning with your payday, to transfer a predetermined amount directly to your savings account. This ensures that saving becomes a top priority, and you are less likely to forget or skip contributions.

Exploring Employer-Sponsored Programs:

If your employer offers retirement plans like 401(k) or 403(b), take advantage of these opportunities for automatic savings. Contribute a percentage of your salary directly to these accounts, and if your employer provides a matching contribution, you are essentially doubling your savings effortlessly.

Utilizing Apps and Fintech Solutions:

In the digital age, there is an array of financial apps and fintech solutions designed to facilitate automatic savings. These apps can round up your purchases to the nearest dollar and save the difference, or they can analyze your spending patterns and save a fixed amount based on your income and expenses. Embrace technology to make saving a seamless part of your daily life.

Gradual Increase in Contributions:

If you're unsure about committing to a high savings rate, start with a modest amount and gradually increase your contributions over time. This approach allows you to adjust to a new budget while still building a consistent saving habit.

Reaping the Benefits of Dollar-Cost Averaging:

Automating your investments is an excellent strategy for long-term wealth building. By contributing a fixed amount regularly to your investment accounts, you practice dollar-cost averaging. This means you buy more shares when prices are low and fewer when prices are high, reducing the impact of market volatility on your overall investment performance.

Staying Informed and Involved:

While automation simplifies the saving process, it's essential to stay informed about your financial progress. Regularly review your savings and investment accounts to track your growth and make necessary adjustments as your financial situation evolves.

Overcoming Temptations:

While automation reduces the temptation to spend impulsively, it's crucial to stay mindful of your financial decisions. Avoid unnecessary debt, prioritize needs over wants, and remain disciplined in sticking to your budget.

By automating your savings, you remove the burden of having to remember to save consistently. This powerful technique not only helps you achieve your short-term and long-term savings goals but also fosters financial discipline and responsibility. Embrace the simplicity of automation, and watch as your savings grow steadily, bringing you closer to a future of financial security and abundance.

Chapter 5: Your Investments

In this chapter, we explore the world of investments, providing you with the knowledge and tools to make informed decisions for your financial future. Discover various investment types, from stocks and bonds to real estate, and learn how to build a successful investment portfolio that aligns with your goals.

• *Overview of Different Investment Types*

We will delve into the diverse world of investments, empowering you to make informed decisions about growing your wealth. Understanding various investment options is crucial to building a robust financial portfolio and achieving your long-term financial objectives. Below is an overview of different investment types to get you started:

Stocks:

Owning shares of a company makes you a partial owner, entitling you to a share of profits and dividends.

Stocks offer potential high returns but also come with higher risks due to market fluctuations.

Bonds:

Bonds are debt securities where investors lend money to governments or corporations in exchange for periodic interest payments.

Bonds are generally considered less risky than stocks, making them suitable for income-focused portfolios.

Mutual Funds:

Mutual funds pool money from multiple investors to invest in a diversified portfolio of stocks, bonds, or other securities.

These funds are managed by professional fund managers, providing easy access to a diverse range of assets.

Exchange-Traded Funds (ETFs):

Similar to mutual funds, ETFs consist of a basket of securities, but they are traded on stock exchanges like individual stocks.

ETFs offer liquidity, lower expense ratios, and flexibility in trading throughout the day.

Real Estate Investment Trusts (REITs):

REITs invest in income-generating real estate properties, such as commercial buildings, apartments, or hotels.

Investors can enjoy potential rental income and property appreciation without directly owning the properties.

Certificates of Deposit (CDs):

CDs are time deposits offered by banks with fixed terms and interest rates.

They are low-risk investments but often have lower returns compared to other assets.

Commodities:

Commodities include physical goods like gold, silver, oil, and agricultural products.

Investing in commodities can serve as a hedge against inflation and provide diversification benefits.

Individual Retirement Accounts (IRAs):

IRAs are tax-advantaged accounts designed for retirement savings, offering various investment options.

Traditional IRAs offer tax-deferred growth, while Roth IRAs provide tax-free withdrawals in retirement.

401(k) and Workplace Retirement Plans:

Employer-sponsored retirement plans, like 401(k)s, allow employees to contribute a portion of their salary before taxes.

Many employers offer matching contributions, which can significantly boost retirement savings.

Cryptocurrencies:

Cryptocurrencies are digital assets that use cryptography for security and operate independently of traditional financial institutions.

Investing in cryptocurrencies carries higher risks due to their volatile nature and evolving regulatory landscape.

Remember, each investment type comes with its own set of risks and rewards. Diversification, or spreading your investments across different assets, is a key strategy to manage risk and optimize returns. As we proceed in this book, we will delve deeper into each investment type, helping you craft a well-balanced investment strategy that aligns with your financial goals and risk tolerance.

Choosing the Right Investments for Your Goals

Now that you have gained an overview of various investment types, it's time to delve into the process of selecting the right investments that align with your financial goals, risk tolerance, and time horizon. This chapter will guide you through the essential considerations and strategies for making informed investment decisions.

Clarify Your Financial Goals:

Start by defining your short-term and long-term financial goals. Are you saving for a down payment on a house, funding your child's education, or planning for a comfortable retirement?

Understanding your goals will help you determine the appropriate investment timeframe and risk level.

Assess Your Risk Tolerance:

Your risk tolerance reflects your comfort level with market fluctuations and the possibility of losing some or all of your investment.

Consider factors like age, financial responsibilities, and your emotional response to market volatility when assessing your risk tolerance.

Diversify Your Portfolio:

Diversification is a fundamental principle of investing. By spreading your investments across different asset classes, industries, and regions, you can reduce risk and enhance potential returns.

Avoid putting all your eggs in one basket; rather, build a well-diversified portfolio that suits your risk appetite and investment goals.

Match Investments to Time Horizon:

Your investment time horizon refers to the period for which you plan to hold an investment before needing the funds for a specific goal.

Longer time horizons allow for more aggressive investment choices, while shorter ones may require more conservative options.

Consider Asset Allocation:

Asset allocation is the distribution of your investments across different asset classes, such as stocks, bonds, and cash.

The right asset allocation depends on your risk tolerance and financial objectives. Younger investors with a long-time horizon may opt for a higher percentage of stocks, while those nearing retirement might favor a more balanced approach.

Analyze Historical Performance:

While past performance doesn't guarantee future results, it can provide insights into an investment's potential.

Research the historical performance of various investment options and evaluate their consistency and volatility over different market conditions.

Factor in Costs and Fees:

Investment costs, such as management fees and expense ratios, can impact your overall returns.

Compare costs across investment vehicles and consider lower-cost options, especially for long-term investments.

Seek Professional Advice:

If you find the investment landscape overwhelming or need personalized guidance, consider consulting a financial advisor.

A qualified advisor can help tailor an investment strategy based on your unique circumstances and financial goals.

Review and Rebalance Periodically:

As your life circumstances change or the market fluctuates, periodically review your portfolio and rebalance if necessary.

Rebalancing involves adjusting your asset allocation to maintain the desired risk level and align with your goals.

Remember that investing is not a one-size-fits-all approach. Your investment strategy should be tailored to your specific goals and circumstances. Be patient and disciplined in your approach and avoid making impulsive decisions based on short-term market movements.

In the next section, we will explore how to get started with investing, providing practical tips and resources to help you take the first steps toward building a successful investment portfolio.

• *Getting Started with Investing*

Congratulations! You have laid the groundwork by understanding different investment types and how to choose the right investments for your goals. Now, let's dive into the practical steps to get started with investing and embark on your journey toward building a secure financial future.

Start Early and Stay Committed:

Time is one of the most valuable assets when it comes to investing. The earlier you start, the more time your investments have to grow through compounding.

Stay committed to your investment strategy and resist the temptation to make frequent changes based on short-term market movements.

Set Clear Investment Goals:

Define your investment objectives and align them with your financial goals, risk tolerance, and time horizon.

Whether you're saving for retirement, funding your child's education, or achieving other milestones, having specific goals will help guide your investment decisions.

Create a Budget for Investing:

Determine how much you can comfortably invest each month after accounting for essential expenses and emergency savings.

Consistently contributing to your investments, even if it's a small amount, can make a significant difference over time.

Understand Your Risk Tolerance:

Be honest about your risk tolerance and choose investments that align with your comfort level.

Remember that all investments carry some degree of risk, and understanding your risk appetite will help you maintain a balanced and stress-free portfolio.

Build a Diversified Portfolio:

Utilize the principle of diversification to spread your investments across different asset classes and industries.

Consider investing in a mix of stocks, bonds, and other assets to reduce overall risk and increase the potential for returns.

Take Advantage of Employer-Sponsored Plans:

If your employer offers a retirement plan, such as a 401(k) or 403(b), take advantage of it, especially if they offer a matching contribution.

Employer matching is essentially free money, so contribute enough to get the full match.

Consider Low-Cost Index Funds and ETFs:

Index funds and ETFs are cost-effective investment options that track the performance of specific market indexes.

They offer instant diversification and generally have lower expense ratios compared to actively managed funds.

Stay Informed and Educated:

Keep yourself informed about financial markets, economic trends, and investment opportunities.

Continuously expand your financial knowledge through books, articles, courses, and reputable financial news sources.

Avoid Emotional Investing:

Emotions can influence investment decisions, leading to impulsive actions that may harm your portfolio.

Stay focused on your long-term goals and avoid making hasty changes based on fear or greed.

Review and Adjust Your Portfolio:

Periodically review your portfolio's performance and make adjustments as needed to stay on track with your goals.

Rebalance your portfolio if your asset allocation deviates significantly from your target allocation.

Seek Professional Guidance:

If you feel overwhelmed or unsure about your investment decisions, consider consulting a certified financial advisor.

A professional can provide personalized advice based on your unique financial situation.

Remember that investing is a journey, and the key to success is staying disciplined, patient, and consistent. Market fluctuations are a natural part of the process, but maintaining a long-term perspective and adhering to your investment strategy will increase your likelihood of achieving your financial goals.

In the next chapter, we will explore retirement planning, discussing the steps to determine how much money you need for retirement and how to achieve your retirement savings goals.

Chapter 6: Your Retirement Planning

In this chapter, we explore the key elements of retirement planning: determining your financial needs, saving strategies, and selecting the ideal retirement plan. Secure your financial future and embrace retirement with confidence and peace of mind.

• *Determining the Amount Needed for Retirement*

As you progress through life, retirement planning becomes an increasingly important aspect of your financial journey. While retirement might seem distant, preparing for it early ensures a comfortable and fulfilling post-working life. One of the key steps in retirement planning is determining the amount of money you'll need to sustain your desired lifestyle during retirement.

Evaluating Your Retirement Lifestyle Goals:

A successful retirement starts with envisioning the lifestyle you want to lead after you stop working. Consider factors such as:

Where do you want to live during retirement?

What kind of activities and hobbies do you wish to pursue?

Will you be traveling frequently or have significant healthcare expenses?

Do you have any specific financial goals or aspirations for your retirement years?

Assessing Current and Expected Expenses:

Analyze your current expenses and estimate how they might change during retirement. While some expenses might decrease, such as work-related costs, others might increase, like healthcare or leisure activities. Take into account potential inflation and the impact it could have on your expenses.

Factoring in Social Security and Other Benefits:

Research the benefits you'll receive from Social Security, pensions, or other retirement plans. Understanding your expected income from these sources will help determine how much additional savings you need to secure your desired retirement lifestyle.

Estimating the Length of Your Retirement:

People are living longer, and a longer lifespan means a longer retirement. Consider your family's health history and plan for the possibility of a retirement that could extend for several decades.

Using the 4% Rule:

One common approach in retirement planning is the 4% rule. It suggests withdrawing approximately 4% of your retirement savings in the first year of retirement and then adjusting subsequent withdrawals for inflation. While this rule can serve as a starting point, individual circumstances and market conditions should also be taken into account.

Seek Professional Advice:

Determining the amount needed for retirement can be complex, and seeking guidance from a financial advisor can prove invaluable. An advisor can help you develop a personalized retirement plan based on your unique financial situation, goals, and risk tolerance.

Regularly Review and Adjust Your Plan:

Life is dynamic, and your retirement plan should be flexible enough to accommodate changes. Regularly review your financial situation and adjust your retirement plan as needed. Consider reassessing your plan whenever significant life events, such as marriage, having children, or changing careers, occur.

Determining the amount needed for retirement is a critical step in achieving financial security and peace of mind during your golden years. By carefully evaluating your retirement lifestyle goals, current and expected expenses, income sources, and using appropriate planning tools, you can lay the groundwork for a successful and enjoyable retirement. Remember, the earlier you start planning and saving, the better positioned you'll be to live a fulfilling life after retirement.

• *Strategies for Saving for Retirement*

Now that you have a clear understanding of how much you'll need for a comfortable retirement, it's time to explore effective strategies to build the necessary savings. Saving for retirement requires discipline, consistency, and a well-thought-out plan. By implementing the following strategies, you can work towards achieving your retirement goals and ensuring financial security in your golden years.

Start Early and Take Advantage of Compound Interest:

Time is your greatest ally when saving for retirement. The earlier you begin, the more time your money has to grow through the power of compound interest. Compound interest allows your investment returns to generate additional returns, snowballing your savings over time. Even small contributions made early in your career can have a substantial impact on your retirement fund.

Contribute to Retirement Accounts:

Take full advantage of tax-advantaged retirement accounts, such as 401(k)s, IRAs (Traditional or Roth), or similar options available in your country. These accounts offer tax benefits and may include employer matching contributions, effectively boosting your savings. Contribute as much as you can afford and aim to maximize your contributions to capitalize on these benefits.

Automate Your Savings:

Set up automatic contributions to your retirement accounts directly from your paycheck. Automating your savings ensures consistent and disciplined saving habits, removing the temptation to spend the money elsewhere. It makes saving for retirement a seamless part of your financial routine.

Increase Contributions with Income Growth:

As your income grows throughout your career, consider increasing your retirement contributions proportionally. This strategy enables you to maintain a consistent standard of living while saving more for the future. Allocate any bonuses, raises, or windfalls to your retirement fund to accelerate your savings.

Live Below Your Means:

Practice frugality and avoid unnecessary expenses. Living below your means allows you to free up more money for retirement savings. Differentiate between needs and wants, and focus on long-term financial security over short-term indulgences.

Diversify Your Investments:

Diversification helps manage risk and optimize returns. Allocate your retirement savings across a mix of assets, such as stocks, bonds, real estate, and other investment vehicles suitable for your risk tolerance and time horizon. A diversified portfolio can help you weather market fluctuations and enhance long-term growth potential.

Stay Informed and Review Your Portfolio Regularly:

Stay updated on market trends and economic conditions. Regularly review your retirement portfolio to ensure it aligns with your goals and risk tolerance. Rebalance your investments as needed to maintain the desired asset allocation.

Consider Delaying Social Security:

If possible, delaying Social Security benefits can result in higher monthly payments during retirement. Each year you delay claiming benefits beyond full retirement age, your monthly benefit increases.

Continuously Educate Yourself:

Stay informed about retirement planning strategies, changes in regulations, and new investment opportunities. A well-informed approach can lead to better decisions for your retirement fund.

Seek Professional Advice:

Consult with a qualified financial advisor who specializes in retirement planning. A professional can assess your unique situation, provide personalized advice, and help optimize your retirement savings plan.

By diligently implementing these strategies and making retirement savings a top priority, you can build a robust financial foundation that leads to a fulfilling and worry-free retirement. Remember that consistency, discipline, and a long-term perspective are the keys to achieving your retirement goals. Begin today, and let your savings grow steadily towards a brighter tomorrow.

• *Selecting the Appropriate Retirement Plan*

As you progress with your retirement planning, choosing the right retirement plan is crucial to ensure your savings are optimized and aligned with your unique financial goals. The options available to you may vary based on your employment status, country of residence, and personal preferences. Exploring the different retirement plans and understanding their benefits can help you make an informed decision that best suits your needs.

Employer-Sponsored Retirement Plans:

Many employers offer retirement plans to their employees, such as 401(k)s in the United States or similar plans in other countries. These plans often come with employer matching contributions, which is essentially "free money" added to your retirement savings. Consider enrolling in your employer's retirement plan as soon as you are eligible to take full advantage of these benefits.

Individual Retirement Accounts (IRAs):

Individual Retirement Accounts (IRAs) are personal retirement savings accounts that offer tax advantages. In the United States, there are two main types of IRAs: Traditional IRAs and Roth IRAs. Traditional IRAs allow for tax-deductible contributions, but withdrawals are taxed in retirement. Roth IRAs, on the other hand, involve contributions with after-tax money, but withdrawals in retirement are generally tax-free. Choose the type of IRA that best aligns with your current and future tax situation.

Self-Employed Retirement Plans:

If you are self-employed or a small business owner, consider retirement plans tailored for your needs, such as a Solo 401(k) or SEP IRA. These plans offer tax advantages similar to employer-sponsored plans and can provide significant opportunities for retirement savings.

Government-Sponsored Retirement Plans:

In some countries, the government offers retirement plans or pension schemes to support citizens during their retirement years. These plans often involve mandatory contributions and provide a baseline income upon retirement. Familiarize yourself with your country's government-sponsored retirement options to understand how they can supplement your personal savings.

Annuities:

Annuities are financial products designed to provide a stream of income during retirement. They can be purchased from insurance companies, and the terms and benefits may vary. Annuities can offer a sense of security by guaranteeing income for life or a specified period, but it's essential to carefully review their terms, fees, and potential tax implications.

Brokerage Accounts:

While not specifically designed for retirement, brokerage accounts can be valuable for additional retirement savings. These accounts offer more flexibility in terms of investment choices but lack the tax advantages of dedicated retirement accounts.

Combination of Retirement Plans:

It's not uncommon for individuals to utilize multiple retirement plans simultaneously. Combining employer-sponsored plans, IRAs, and other investment accounts can create a diversified retirement portfolio and optimize your savings potential.

Seek Professional Guidance:

Retirement planning can be complex, and seeking advice from a certified financial advisor or retirement specialist is advisable. An experienced professional can help you navigate the various retirement plan options, understand tax implications, and create a comprehensive retirement strategy tailored to your specific needs.

Remember that selecting the appropriate retirement plan is a significant decision with long-term consequences. Take the time to research and analyze the available options and seek professional guidance to ensure your retirement plan aligns with your financial goals and provides a secure and comfortable future.

Chapter 7: Your Debt Management

In this chapter, we'll explore effective strategies for handling debt responsibly, helping you achieve financial stability and build a stronger credit profile. Learn how to tackle student loans, credit card debt, and other financial liabilities to move closer to your financial freedom.

• *Understanding Different Types of Debt*

Debt is a crucial aspect of personal finance that can significantly impact your financial health. When managed wisely, it can be a useful tool for achieving financial goals, such as purchasing a home or funding education. However, mismanagement of debt can lead to financial struggles and hinder your ability to build wealth. We will explore the various types of debt and learn how to make informed decisions regarding borrowing and repayment.

Section A: Good Debt vs. Bad Debt

Defining Good Debt: Some types of debt can be considered "good" because they can potentially generate long-term benefits or asset appreciation. We'll discuss examples such as:

a. Mortgage loans and real estate investments

b. Student loans for education and skill enhancement

c. Small business loans for entrepreneurial ventures

Identifying Bad Debt: Certain types of debt are often considered "bad" as they typically involve high-interest rates and depreciating assets. We'll delve into examples such as:

a. Credit card debt and its impact on financial health

b. Payday loans and their associated risks

c. Impulse purchases and the danger of accumulating consumer debt

Section B: Secured vs. Unsecured Debt

Understanding Secured Debt: Secured debt is backed by collateral, providing lenders with a level of security. We'll explore:

a. The benefits and risks associated with secured loans

b. Examples of secured debt, including car loans and home equity loans

c. The consequences of defaulting on secured loans

Unpacking Unsecured Debt: Unsecured debt does not require collateral and is usually based on the borrower's creditworthiness. We'll cover:

a. Types of unsecured debt, like credit cards and personal loans

b. The importance of credit scores and their impact on interest rates

c. Strategies for managing unsecured debt responsibly.

Section C: Fixed vs. Variable Interest Rates

Grasping Fixed Interest Rates: With fixed-rate loans, the interest remains constant throughout the loan term. We'll discuss:

a. The predictability and stability of fixed-rate loans

b. Common examples of fixed-rate loans, such as fixed-rate mortgages

c. The pros and cons of choosing fixed interest rates.

Navigating Variable Interest Rates: Variable-rate loans have fluctuating interest rates tied to market conditions. We'll explore:

a. The flexibility and potential risks of variable-rate loans

b. Examples of variable-rate debt, including adjustable-rate mortgages

c. How to manage and prepare for changes in variable interest rates.

Section D: Strategies for Debt Management and Repayment

Debt Consolidation: Understanding the concept of consolidating multiple debts into a single loan for easier management and potential interest savings.

Debt Snowball vs. Debt Avalanche: Comparing two popular debt repayment strategies and determining which may be more suitable for your financial situation.

Avoiding Excessive Debt: Tips and techniques for staying cautious about taking on new debt and living within your means.

Understanding the various types of debt is crucial for making sound financial decisions. By differentiating between good and bad debt and comprehending secured versus unsecured loans, you can effectively manage your borrowing and repayment strategies. Additionally, grasping the concept of fixed and variable interest rates equips you with the knowledge to navigate the borrowing landscape successfully. Armed with this understanding, you can work towards a debt-free future and improve your overall financial well-being.

• *How to Manage and Reduce Debt*

Debt can quickly become overwhelming, but with a proactive approach and disciplined financial habits, you can effectively manage and reduce your debt burden. In this section, we'll explore practical strategies and actionable steps to take control of your debts and work towards becoming debt-free.

Assessing Your Debt Situation

Creating a Detailed Debt Inventory: List all your debts, including outstanding balances, interest rates, and minimum monthly payments. This inventory will serve as a clear picture of your debt landscape.

Analyzing Your Cash Flow: Evaluate your income and expenses to understand how much money is available for debt repayment. Identifying potential areas to cut expenses can free up more funds to put towards debt reduction.

Prioritizing Debt Repayment

The Debt Snowball Method: Start by paying off your smallest debt first while making minimum payments on other debts. As each debt is paid off, redirect the funds to tackle the next smallest debt. This approach provides a sense of accomplishment and motivation as debts are eliminated one by one.

The Debt Avalanche Method: Focus on paying off debts with the highest interest rates first. This method can save you more money in interest payments over time but may require more patience to see significant progress on larger debts.

Negotiating with Creditors

Communicating with Creditors: If you're facing financial hardship, consider reaching out to your creditors to negotiate more manageable payment terms or interest rates. Many lenders are willing to work with you to avoid default and charge-offs.

Exploring Debt Consolidation

Consolidation Loans: If you have multiple high-interest debts, a consolidation loan can combine them into a single loan with a lower interest rate. This simplifies debt management and may reduce your monthly payments.

Balance Transfer Credit Cards: Transfer high-interest credit card balances to a card with a promotional 0% interest rate. Utilize the interest-free period to aggressively pay down the balance.

Seeking Professional Guidance

Credit Counseling Services: Non-profit credit counseling agencies can provide guidance and support to help you create a realistic debt repayment plan.

Debt Management Plans: With the assistance of a credit counselor, enroll in a debt management plan that consolidates your debts and establishes a structured repayment schedule.

Avoiding Accumulating New Debt

Adopting Responsible Spending Habits: Develop a budget and stick to it, avoiding unnecessary expenses and impulse purchases.

Building an Emergency Fund: Having an emergency fund ensures you're prepared for unexpected expenses and reduces the need to rely on credit cards or loans in times of financial strain.

Managing and reducing debt requires determination, discipline, and a well-thought-out plan. By assessing your debt situation, prioritizing repayment, and exploring consolidation options, you can take control of your finances and work towards becoming debt-free. Remember that seeking professional guidance is always an option if you find yourself overwhelmed. By adopting responsible spending habits and building an emergency fund, you can not only manage your current debt but also establish a strong foundation for a debt-free and financially secure future. With these tools and strategies in hand, you'll be on your way to achieving greater financial freedom and living a richer life.

• *Strategies for Paying off Loans Efficiently*

As you embark on your journey to become debt-free, adopting effective strategies for paying off loans efficiently can accelerate your progress and save you money in interest payments. In this section, we'll explore tried-and-true methods to tackle your debts strategically and achieve financial freedom sooner.

Make Extra Payments Whenever Possible

Utilize Windfalls: Use unexpected bonuses, tax refunds, or monetary gifts to make additional payments on your loans. This infusion of cash can make a significant dent in your outstanding balance.

Implement Bi-Weekly Payments: Split your monthly loan payment in half and make payments every two weeks. By the end of the year, you'll have made one extra month's payment, reducing both the principal balance and overall interest paid.

Apply the Snowflake Method

Put Unexpected Funds to Work: Whenever you receive small amounts of money, like cashback rewards, refunds, or spare change, apply them directly to your loan. These seemingly insignificant amounts, known as "snowflakes," can accumulate and contribute to debt reduction.

Target High-Interest Debt First

Focus on Paying Off High-Rate Loans: Allocate more funds towards loans with the highest interest rates first. This approach minimizes the amount of interest accumulating and enables you to repay the costliest debt more quickly.

Consider Loan Refinancing

Explore Lower Interest Rates: If your credit score has improved since obtaining your loans, explore the possibility of refinancing to secure lower interest rates. Refinancing can lead to substantial savings on interest payments over the life of the loan.

Use the Debt Avalanche Method

Organize Debt by Interest Rate: List your debts in descending order based on interest rates. Allocate the majority of your debt repayment funds to the highest interest rate loan while making minimum payments on others. Once the highest interest loan is paid off, move on to the next highest interest rate, and so on.

Negotiate with Lenders

Request Lower Interest Rates: Contact your lenders and inquire about the possibility of lowering your interest rates. Explain your financial situation and demonstrate a commitment to repaying the loan promptly. Some lenders may be willing to reduce your rate, especially if you have a good repayment history.

Stay Motivated and Celebrate Milestones

Set Short-Term Goals: Break your debt repayment journey into smaller, achievable goals. Celebrate each milestone reached, whether it's paying off a specific debt or reaching a certain percentage of overall debt reduction.

Find Support: Share your financial goals with friends, family, or online communities. Surrounding yourself with a supportive network can help keep you motivated and accountable.

Paying off loans efficiently requires dedication, perseverance, and a well-executed plan. By implementing extra payments, the snowflake method, and the debt avalanche strategy, you can expedite the debt repayment process and save money on interest. Consider loan refinancing as a viable option to secure lower interest rates and explore negotiation tactics with lenders. Setting short-term goals and finding support can keep you motivated throughout your journey to financial freedom. With these strategies in your arsenal, you'll be well on your way to achieving your goal of becoming debt-free and living a richer life. Remember, every step towards reducing debt brings you closer to financial independence and opens the door to new opportunities.

• *Tips for Improving Credit Scores*

Your credit score plays a critical role in your financial life, affecting your ability to secure loans, obtain favorable interest rates, and even rent an apartment or get a job. A higher credit score can lead to significant financial advantages, making it essential to adopt habits that improve your creditworthiness. In this section, we'll explore practical tips to enhance your credit score and set you on a path to better financial opportunities.

Check Your Credit Report Regularly

Obtain Free Credit Reports: Request a free credit report from each of the three major credit bureaus (Equifax, Experian, and TransUnion) annually. Review the reports for errors, inaccuracies, or signs of identity theft.

Dispute Errors: If you find any discrepancies or inaccuracies in your credit report, dispute them promptly with the respective credit bureau to have them corrected.

Pay Bills on Time

Timely Payments Matter: Paying your bills on time is one of the most influential factors in determining your credit score. Set up reminders or automatic payments to ensure you never miss a due date.

Reduce Credit Card Balances

Lower Credit Utilization: Aim to keep your credit card balances below 30% of your credit limit. High credit utilization can negatively impact your credit score.

Prioritize High-Interest Cards: If possible, focus on paying off credit cards with the highest interest rates first. Reducing credit card balances can lead to a quick improvement in your credit score.

Avoid Opening Unnecessary Credit Accounts

Be Selective with New Accounts: Each time you apply for new credit, it generates a hard inquiry on your credit report, which can temporarily lower your credit score. Only apply for credit when necessary and avoid multiple credit applications within a short period.

Keep Old Accounts Open

Length of Credit History Matters: The age of your credit accounts affects your credit score. Keeping older accounts open demonstrates a longer credit history, which can positively impact your creditworthiness.

Diversify Your Credit Mix

Types of Credit Matter: Having a mix of credit accounts, such as credit cards, installment loans, and retail accounts, can positively influence your credit score. However, only open accounts you genuinely need and can manage responsibly.

Become an Authorized User

Piggyback on Positive Accounts: If a family member or friend with a strong credit history is willing to add you as an authorized user on their credit card, their positive payment history can benefit your credit score.

Be Patient and Persistent

Building Credit Takes Time: Improving your credit score is not an overnight process. Stay committed to responsible financial habits, and your credit score will gradually rise over time.

Improving your credit score is a fundamental step in achieving financial success. By regularly checking your credit report, paying bills on time, reducing credit card balances, and being selective with new credit accounts, you can enhance your creditworthiness and open doors to better financial opportunities. Keeping old accounts open, diversifying your credit mix, and becoming an authorized user on a positive account can further bolster your credit score. Remember that building credit takes time and persistence, but with dedication and these essential tips, you can set yourself on a path to a stronger financial future. A higher credit score not only makes borrowing easier and more affordable but also empowers you to achieve your financial goals and live a richer life.

Chapter 8: Your Tax Strategy

As you embark on your journey toward financial success, one crucial aspect that often goes overlooked but holds immense significance is tax planning. Taxes are an inevitable part of our financial lives, and understanding how they impact our finances can make a substantial difference in achieving our financial goals. In this chapter, we will explore the importance of tax planning, how it affects your overall financial picture, and strategies to optimize your tax situation legally and ethically.

• *The Importance of Tax Planning*

When it comes to managing our finances, tax planning is an integral and often overlooked aspect of achieving financial success. Taxes play a significant role in our financial lives, and a lack of proper tax planning can lead to missed opportunities and unnecessary financial burdens. We will explore the importance of tax planning and how it can positively impact your overall financial well-being.

A. Understanding the Complexity of Taxes

The world of taxes can be intricate and overwhelming, with various tax laws, deductions, credits, and exemptions constantly evolving. Without a clear understanding of these complexities, individuals may inadvertently overpay their taxes or miss out on potential savings. Tax planning provides the necessary knowledge and strategies to navigate through these intricacies and ensure that you are maximizing your tax benefits while remaining compliant with the law.

B. Maximizing Tax Deductions and Credits

One of the key objectives of tax planning is to identify and take advantage of eligible tax deductions and credits. Tax deductions reduce your taxable income, while tax credits directly reduce your tax liability. Through careful planning and consideration of your financial situation, you can potentially lower the amount of taxes you owe, putting more money back into your pocket. Whether it's deducting qualified business expenses, educational expenses, or contributions to retirement accounts, understanding the available deductions and credits can significantly impact your tax return.

C. Exploring Tax-Efficient Investment Strategies

Investing is an essential component of building wealth, and tax planning can optimize your investment strategy. By strategically placing your investments in tax-efficient accounts, such as IRAs (Individual Retirement Accounts) or 401(k)s, you can minimize the tax implications of your earnings and capital gains. Additionally, understanding the tax consequences of different investment vehicles, such as stocks, bonds, and mutual funds, will enable you to make informed decisions that align with your financial goals and tax situation.

D. Understanding the Impact of Taxes on Your Financial Goals

Taxes can have a substantial impact on your ability to achieve financial goals, such as buying a home, funding your children's education, or saving for retirement. Effective tax planning allows you to structure your financial decisions in a way that optimizes tax benefits and ensures your resources are allocated efficiently. Whether it involves timing significant financial transactions or using tax-advantaged accounts, having a proactive tax strategy can mean the difference between reaching your goals and falling short.

E. Minimizing Tax-Related Stress and Uncertainty

Tax season can be a source of stress and uncertainty for many individuals. Without proper planning, gathering necessary documents, filing tax returns, and dealing with potential audits can be overwhelming. Tax planning offers peace of mind by providing a clear roadmap and reducing the stress associated with financial uncertainties. When you have a well-thought-out tax plan in place, you can approach tax season with confidence, knowing that you have taken the necessary steps to minimize tax-related surprises.

Tax planning is an essential tool for achieving financial success and stability. By understanding the complexity of taxes, maximizing deductions and credits, exploring tax-efficient investment strategies, and aligning your financial goals with tax implications, you can make the most of your hard-earned money. Additionally, tax planning reduces stress and uncertainty, allowing you to focus on other aspects of your financial journey. With a proactive approach to tax planning, you can navigate the ever-changing tax landscape with confidence and ensure that you are on track to make more, save more, and live richer.

• *Maximizing Tax Deductions and Credits*

A crucial aspect of effective tax planning is understanding the various tax deductions and credits available to taxpayers. These valuable opportunities can significantly reduce your taxable income and tax liability, ultimately leading to substantial savings. In this section, we will delve deeper into the world of tax deductions and credits, equipping you with the knowledge to optimize your tax return.

Tax Deductions: Reducing Your Taxable Income

Tax deductions are expenses, contributions, or allowances that the tax code allows you to subtract from your gross income, resulting in a lower taxable income. By maximizing your deductions, you can shrink the portion of your income that is subject to taxation. Here are some common deductions you might be eligible for:

a. Standard Deduction: The standard deduction is a fixed amount that all taxpayers can claim without itemizing their deductions. The standard deduction can vary depending on your filing status and is often adjusted each tax year to account for inflation.

b. Itemized Deductions: Alternatively, you can choose to itemize your deductions if they exceed the standard deduction. Itemized deductions encompass a wide range of expenses, including:

State and local taxes

Mortgage interest and property taxes

Medical expenses (subject to certain limitations)

Charitable contributions

Unreimbursed job-related expenses

Certain educational expenses

Casualty and theft losses

Tax Credits: Direct Reduction of Tax Liability

Tax credits are even more valuable than deductions, as they directly reduce your tax liability dollar-for-dollar. By claiming tax credits, you effectively reduce the amount of taxes you owe, providing significant savings. Here are some common tax credits you might be eligible for:

a. Child Tax Credit: If you have qualifying children, you may be eligible for the Child Tax Credit, which can provide substantial relief for families. The credit amount can vary based on the number of children and your income.

b. Earned Income Tax Credit (EITC): The EITC is designed to assist low to moderate-income individuals and families. Depending on your income and family size, this credit can be quite generous and may result in a refund even if you had no tax liability.

c. Education Credits: The American Opportunity Credit and the Lifetime Learning Credit are available to help offset the costs of higher education. These credits can be claimed for qualified tuition and related expenses.

d. Renewable Energy Credits: Investing in renewable energy sources, such as solar panels or wind turbines, can make you eligible for certain tax credits that encourage sustainable practices.

Timing Strategies: Managing Deductions and Credits

An essential aspect of tax planning involves timing certain expenses and transactions to maximize deductions and credits. For example:

a. Bundling Deductions: If you have the option to control the timing of deductible expenses, consider bundling them into a single tax year to exceed the standard deduction and itemize.

b. Charitable Contributions: Strategically timing charitable donations can help you optimize your deductions. Consider bunching contributions in a single tax year or utilizing donor-advised funds to make larger donations while still retaining the ability to distribute them over time.

c. Retirement Contributions: Contributing to tax-advantaged retirement accounts, such as Traditional IRAs or 401(k)s, can reduce your taxable income while simultaneously building your retirement savings.

d. Education Expenses: Timing the payment of educational expenses to fall within the tax year can make you eligible for education-related tax credits.

Seek Professional Advice

Given the complexity of tax laws and regulations, seeking advice from a qualified tax professional is essential to ensure that you are taking advantage of all available deductions and credits. Tax professionals can provide personalized guidance tailored to your unique financial situation, ensuring that you optimize your tax return and avoid costly mistakes.

Maximizing tax deductions and credits is a fundamental component of effective tax planning. By understanding the various deductions and credits available to you, strategically timing expenses, and seeking professional advice, you can significantly reduce your tax burden and keep more of your hard-earned money. As you navigate the world of tax planning, remember that staying informed and proactive is key to making the most of the tax benefits available to you. By incorporating these strategies into your financial planning, you can move closer to achieving financial success and living a more abundant life.

• *Exploring Tax-Efficient Investment Strategies*

Investing is a powerful tool for growing your wealth and achieving your financial goals. However, the tax implications of different investment choices can significantly impact your overall returns. To optimize your investment strategy, it's essential to explore tax-efficient investment strategies. In this section, we will delve into various approaches that can help you minimize the taxes you pay on your investment earnings.

Utilizing Tax-Advantaged Accounts

One of the most effective ways to achieve tax efficiency in investing is by utilizing tax-advantaged accounts. These accounts offer tax benefits that can help you grow your investments faster and defer taxes to a later date. Common tax-advantaged accounts include:

a. Individual Retirement Accounts (IRAs): Traditional IRAs and Roth IRAs offer unique tax advantages. Contributions to Traditional IRAs may be tax-deductible, reducing your taxable income for the current year. Roth IRA contributions are made with after-tax dollars, but qualified withdrawals are tax-free in retirement.

b. Employer-Sponsored Retirement Plans: If your employer offers a 401(k) or similar retirement plan, take advantage of it. Contributions to these plans are made with pre-tax dollars, reducing your taxable income, and earnings grow tax-deferred until withdrawal.

c. Health Savings Accounts (HSAs): HSAs are triple-tax-advantaged accounts designed for medical expenses. Contributions are tax-deductible, growth is tax-free, and withdrawals for qualified medical expenses are also tax-free.

Tax Loss Harvesting

Tax loss harvesting is a strategy used to offset capital gains taxes by selling investments that have decreased in value (realizing losses). These losses can then be used to offset capital gains realized from other investments. If losses exceed gains, you can deduct up to $3,000 of the excess loss against other income. Any remaining losses can be carried forward to offset future gains.

Buy and Hold Strategy

Frequent trading within taxable accounts can trigger capital gains taxes, reducing your overall returns. A buy-and-hold strategy involves investing in quality assets for the long term, minimizing the number of taxable events. By holding investments for over a year, you can qualify for long-term capital gains tax rates, which are generally lower than short-term rates.

Asset Location

Strategically placing your investments across different types of accounts can also contribute to tax efficiency. High-growth, high-tax investments are best held in tax-advantaged accounts, while lower-growth, tax-efficient investments may be suitable for taxable accounts.

Qualified Dividends and Long-Term Capital Gains

Investing in assets that generate qualified dividends and long-term capital gains can lead to tax advantages. Qualified dividends and long-term capital gains are typically taxed at lower rates than ordinary income, providing an opportunity for tax savings.

Tax-Aware Portfolio Rebalancing

As your investment portfolio grows and changes, rebalancing becomes necessary to maintain your desired asset allocation. Tax-aware portfolio rebalancing involves considering the tax consequences of selling and buying assets. By prioritizing tax-efficient transactions, you can minimize the impact of taxes while aligning your portfolio with your long-term goals.

Consult with a Financial Advisor

The world of tax-efficient investing can be complex, and seeking advice from a qualified financial advisor can be immensely beneficial. A financial advisor can help you design a personalized investment strategy that takes into account your financial goals, risk tolerance, and tax situation. They can also keep you informed about changes in tax laws and regulations that may affect your investments.

Tax-efficient investment strategies play a vital role in preserving and growing your wealth. By utilizing tax-advantaged accounts, engaging in tax loss harvesting, employing a buy-and-hold strategy, and strategically locating assets, you can optimize your investment returns while minimizing your tax burden. Remember that tax-efficient investing is a long-term approach, and staying proactive and well-informed will ensure that you make the most of your investment opportunities. As you explore tax-efficient strategies, you move closer to achieving financial success and securing a brighter financial future.

• *Understanding the Impact of Taxes on Your Financial Goals*

As you work diligently towards achieving your financial goals, it's essential to recognize the significant role that taxes play in shaping your financial journey. The impact of taxes can influence the growth of your investments, the amount of money available for spending, and the overall success of your financial plans. In this section, we will explore the profound impact that taxes can have on your financial goals and the strategies you can employ to align your tax planning with your aspirations.

Tax Drag: The Erosion of Investment Returns

Taxes can impose a drag on your investment returns, potentially reducing the growth of your portfolio over time. Depending on your tax bracket and the type of investments you hold, you may owe taxes on dividends, interest, and capital gains. The more taxable events occur within your portfolio, the more significant the tax drag becomes. Understanding the tax implications of your investments can help you make informed decisions and mitigate this effect.

Inflation and Taxation

Inflation erodes the purchasing power of money over time, and taxes can exacerbate its impact. For example, if your investments earn a 6% return and you are taxed at a 20% rate, your real return after taxes would be 4.8%. This decrease in real return may not keep pace with inflation, leading to reduced purchasing power and potentially hindering your financial goals. Factoring in taxes and inflation when setting financial targets is essential to ensure that your goals remain achievable.

Tax-Efficient Goal Planning

Tailoring your investment strategies to align with your specific financial goals can enhance tax efficiency. Short-term goals, such as a vacation or a down payment on a house, might benefit from tax-efficient investments to preserve the principal and minimize tax liabilities. Long-term goals, such as retirement, may require a combination of tax-advantaged accounts and tax-efficient investments to optimize growth while minimizing tax burdens.

Tax Diversification

Similar to diversifying your investment portfolio, tax diversification involves spreading your assets across various tax-advantaged and taxable accounts. This approach can offer flexibility in managing your tax liability in retirement. By having a mix of taxable and tax-advantaged funds, you can strategically withdraw from accounts to minimize your tax burden during different phases of retirement.

Managing Required Minimum Distributions (RMDs)

For certain tax-advantaged retirement accounts like Traditional IRAs and 401(k)s, the IRS requires you to start taking minimum distributions upon reaching a certain age. These Required Minimum Distributions (RMDs) can impact your tax situation in retirement. Understanding the timing and impact of RMDs allows you to plan accordingly to minimize any adverse tax consequences.

Adjusting Tax Strategies for Life Changes

Major life events, such as marriage, having children, or changing jobs, can significantly affect your tax situation. When these changes occur, it is crucial to reassess your tax strategies and adjust them accordingly. Filing status, dependents, and income levels can all influence your tax liability, and adapting your approach can lead to tax savings.

Ongoing Review and Adaptation

The tax landscape is continuously evolving, with changes in tax laws and regulations occurring regularly. As such, it is essential to review your tax strategies periodically and adapt them to current circumstances. Consulting with a tax professional or financial advisor can help you stay informed and make necessary adjustments to optimize your tax planning.

Understanding the impact of taxes on your financial goals is paramount to successful tax planning. By recognizing the tax drag on investments, factoring in inflation and taxation, employing tax-efficient goal planning, and implementing tax diversification, you can align your tax strategy with your aspirations. Additionally, staying vigilant in managing RMDs and adjusting your tax approach to life changes will help ensure that your tax planning remains effective over time. As you navigate the complex terrain of taxes, you are better equipped to pursue your financial goals and create a more prosperous future.

Chapter 9: Your Insurance Coverage

In this chapter, we delve into a crucial aspect of financial planning that often receives inadequate attention – insurance coverage. Safeguarding your financial well-being and that of your loved ones is paramount, and insurance plays a pivotal role in providing protection and peace of mind. From life and health to home and auto insurance, understanding the significance of insurance in your financial journey is fundamental. By exploring the various types of insurance policies available, evaluating your specific needs, and implementing strategic measures to minimize risks, you can fortify your financial foundation and be better prepared to face life's uncertainties.

• *Importance of Insurance in Financial Planning*

Insurance acts as a shield, guarding you against unexpected setbacks and potential financial burdens that may arise due to unforeseen circumstances. It is the safety net that cushions your finances during difficult times, ensuring that you and your loved ones are protected from devastating losses. While many individuals often overlook insurance in their financial planning, its significance cannot be overstated.

Protection of Assets and Wealth: Your financial security is intertwined with the assets you've acquired and the wealth you've built over time. Whether it's your home, car, business, or personal belongings, having appropriate insurance coverage shields these valuable assets from damage, theft, or natural disasters. In the event of an unfortunate incident, insurance provides the means to rebuild and recover without depleting your savings or disrupting your financial goals.

Safeguarding Your Health and Well-being: Your health is undoubtedly your most valuable asset. Health insurance offers vital protection by covering medical expenses, hospitalization costs, and treatments, allowing you to access quality healthcare without the burden of exorbitant bills. A comprehensive health insurance plan ensures that you receive the care you need while preserving your financial stability.

Financial Protection for Loved Ones: Life insurance holds a special place in financial planning, especially when you have dependents relying on your income. It provides financial support to your family in the unfortunate event of your passing, enabling them to cover living expenses, mortgage payments, educational needs, and other essential costs. Life insurance ensures that your loved ones can maintain their quality of life even in your absence.

Managing Liabilities and Debts: In today's world, it is common to have various financial obligations, such as mortgages, student loans, or credit card debt. Insurance can serve as a safety net that helps cover these debts if unexpected circumstances prevent you from meeting your financial commitments. This protects both your assets and your loved ones from potential financial burdens.

Minimizing Business Risks: For entrepreneurs and business owners, insurance is essential for safeguarding their enterprises from unforeseen challenges. Business insurance can cover property damage, liability claims, employee-related risks, and other potential threats that could disrupt the business's operations or financial stability.

Insurance is an integral component of sound financial planning. It offers protection, security, and stability in the face of life's uncertainties. By identifying your specific insurance needs, selecting appropriate coverage, and regularly reviewing your policies, you can confidently pursue your financial goals with the assurance that you have taken prudent steps to protect your wealth, health, and future. Remember, insurance is not just an expense but an invaluable investment in your financial well-being.

- ## *Evaluating and Choosing the Right Insurance Policies (life, health, home, auto, etc.)*

As you embark on the journey of securing your financial future, one of the most critical steps in the insurance planning process is evaluating and selecting the right insurance policies. Each insurance type serves a specific purpose, and understanding the nuances of different policies is essential to ensure comprehensive coverage tailored to your unique needs. In this chapter, we will explore the key considerations when evaluating life, health, home, auto, and other insurance options, empowering you to make informed decisions that provide maximum protection and value for your hard-earned money.

Assessing Your Needs: Before delving into the intricacies of insurance policies, it's crucial to assess your current financial situation, personal circumstances, and future goals. Ask yourself pertinent questions, such as:

What are your primary financial responsibilities, and who depends on your income?

Do you have dependents, and if so, what are their financial needs in the event of your absence?

What are the potential risks you may face, such as health issues, property damage, or liability claims?

What assets do you own, and what level of protection do they require?

Understanding your specific requirements will form the foundation for selecting appropriate insurance policies that align with your unique situation.

Life Insurance Options: Life insurance provides financial security to your loved ones in the event of your passing, offering several types of policies to consider:

Term Life Insurance: Provides coverage for a specific period (term) and pays out a death benefit if you pass away during that term. It's a cost-effective option for temporary protection.

Whole Life Insurance: Offers lifetime coverage and includes a cash value component that grows over time. It can act as a long-term investment and provides permanent protection.

Universal Life Insurance: Combines life coverage with a flexible savings component, allowing you to adjust premiums and death benefits as your financial situation evolves.

Variable Life Insurance: Offers investment options within the policy, allowing you to allocate cash value among various investment vehicles.

Selecting the right life insurance policy involves balancing affordability, coverage duration, and long-term financial goals.

Health Insurance Considerations: Health insurance is essential for managing medical expenses and maintaining good health. When evaluating health insurance policies, consider the following:

Coverage Scope: Assess the extent of coverage, including doctor visits, hospitalization, prescription drugs, and preventive care.

Network Providers: Ensure your preferred healthcare providers are part of the insurance network to access quality care without out-of-network costs.

Deductibles and Premiums: Evaluate the trade-off between monthly premiums and deductibles to strike the right balance between affordability and coverage.

Home Insurance Essentials: Home insurance protects one of your most significant investments – your property. When choosing a home insurance policy, pay attention to:

Coverage Types: Determine whether you need basic dwelling coverage or additional protection for personal belongings, liability, and temporary living expenses.

Policy Limits: Ensure that the coverage limits adequately reflect the value of your property and possessions.

Deductibles: Consider your ability to pay the deductible in the event of a claim and select a suitable amount.

Auto Insurance Factors: Auto insurance is crucial for safeguarding against accidents and vehicle-related risks. When assessing auto insurance options, focus on:

Liability Coverage: Evaluate the coverage limits for bodily injury and property damage to comply with legal requirements and protect your assets.

Comprehensive and Collision Coverage: Determine if comprehensive coverage (for non-collision incidents) and collision coverage (for accidents) are necessary based on your vehicle's value and your risk tolerance.

Discounts and Deductibles: Inquire about available discounts, such as safe driver discounts or multi-policy discounts, and choose deductibles that align with your budget.

Additional Insurance Considerations: Depending on your lifestyle and financial situation, you may require other insurance policies, such as disability insurance, long-term care insurance, umbrella insurance, or business insurance. Evaluate these options based on your specific needs and potential risks.

Review and Periodic Adjustments: Life is dynamic, and so are your insurance needs. Regularly review your policies, particularly during significant life events like marriage, the birth of a child, or changes in employment or assets. Ensure your coverage aligns with your evolving circumstances and financial goals.

Evaluating and choosing the right insurance policies is a pivotal aspect of comprehensive financial planning. By conducting a thorough assessment of your needs, understanding the different types of insurance available, and customizing your coverage accordingly, you can build a robust insurance portfolio that provides the protection and peace of mind you and your loved ones deserve. Remember, the right insurance policies serve as a strong safety net, ensuring that your hard work and aspirations remain secure even in the face of life's uncertainties.

• *Strategies for Minimizing Insurance Costs*

While insurance is an indispensable part of a solid financial plan, it's natural to seek ways to minimize insurance costs without compromising on the level of protection you need. By adopting smart strategies and making informed choices, you can optimize your insurance coverage and reduce premiums, making insurance more affordable and efficient. In this chapter, we will explore various tactics to help you save on insurance costs while still maintaining adequate coverage.

Comparison Shopping: The first step to cost-effective insurance is comparing quotes from different insurance providers. Request multiple quotes for the same level of coverage to identify competitive pricing and potential discounts. Online comparison tools and independent insurance agents can be valuable resources to simplify this process.

Bundling Policies: Many insurance companies offer discounts for bundling multiple policies, such as combining auto and home insurance or adding life insurance to your existing coverage. Bundling can lead to significant savings while streamlining your insurance management.

Raising Deductibles: Increasing your deductibles can lower your insurance premiums. However, ensure that you can comfortably afford the higher out-of-pocket expenses if you need to file a claim. Maintaining an emergency fund can help cover unexpected deductibles.

Maintaining a Good Credit Score: Your credit score can impact your insurance rates, as insurers often use credit-based insurance scores to assess risk. Maintaining a good credit score by managing debts responsibly and paying bills on time can lead to lower insurance premiums.

Driving Safely: If you have auto insurance, practicing safe driving habits can earn you discounts and lower premiums. Many insurers offer rewards for accident-free records and taking defensive driving courses.

Installing Security Systems: For home insurance, installing security systems and fire alarms can qualify you for lower rates. These measures reduce the risk of theft and property damage, making you less of a liability to the insurer.

Reviewing Coverage Annually: Regularly review your insurance policies and coverage limits to ensure they still align with your needs and circumstances. As your life changes, you may find that you can adjust your coverage, which may result in lower costs.

Utilizing Insurance Discounts: Inquire about available discounts, as insurers often offer various cost-saving opportunities. Common discounts include multi-policy discounts, safe driver discounts, low mileage discounts for auto insurance, and non-smoker discounts for life insurance.

Considering Higher Insurance Deductibles: For health insurance, consider a high-deductible health plan (HDHP) paired with a Health Savings Account (HSA). HDHPs typically have lower premiums, and HSAs offer tax advantages for medical expenses.

Regularly Reevaluating Insurance Needs: As your life evolves, your insurance needs may change. Periodically reevaluating your insurance coverage ensures you're not paying for unnecessary or inadequate protection.

Quitting Tobacco Use: If you're a smoker, quitting can significantly reduce life insurance costs. Insurers often charge higher premiums for smokers due to increased health risks associated with tobacco use.

Choosing the Right Insurance Policy: Opting for the insurance policy that best suits your needs and lifestyle can prevent you from paying for coverage you don't require. Tailoring your insurance choices can optimize both protection and costs.

By implementing these strategies, you can strike a balance between sufficient insurance coverage and affordability, making the most of your insurance investment. Remember, while cost-saving measures are valuable, ensuring that you have the right coverage to protect your financial security remains the ultimate goal. As your circumstances change, it's essential to reassess your insurance plans periodically to stay on track with your evolving financial objectives.

• *Understanding and Managing Risk Effectively*

Risk is an inherent part of life, and in the realm of personal finance, managing risk effectively is essential to safeguard your financial well-being. Insurance serves as a crucial tool in mitigating various risks but understanding the different types of risks and implementing comprehensive risk management strategies go hand in hand with a robust financial plan. In this chapter, we will explore the concept of risk, identify common risks individuals face, and delve into strategies to manage and minimize their impact on your financial future.

Understanding Risk: Risk refers to the possibility of an event occurring that could have adverse consequences on your financial goals and assets. Financial risks come in various forms, including:

Market Risk: The potential for investment values to fluctuate due to changes in market conditions.

Credit Risk: The likelihood of borrowers defaulting on loans, leading to financial losses for lenders.

Inflation Risk: The risk of your purchasing power decreasing over time due to rising inflation rates.

Longevity Risk: The risk of outliving your financial resources during retirement.

Property and Casualty Risk: The risk of damage or loss to your property due to natural disasters, accidents, or theft.

Health and Long-Term Care Risk: The risk of facing significant medical expenses or the need for long-term care services.

Diversification: Diversifying your investments is a fundamental risk management strategy. By spreading your investments across different asset classes and sectors, you can reduce the impact of a single investment's poor performance on your overall portfolio.

Asset Allocation: Determining the appropriate mix of assets in your investment portfolio is crucial for managing risk. Balancing higher-risk, higher-reward investments with more stable, low-risk assets can align with your risk tolerance and financial goals.

Emergency Fund: Maintaining an emergency fund acts as a safety net for unexpected events, such as job loss or medical emergencies. Having three to six months' worth of living expenses in a liquid account can provide financial security during challenging times.

Insurance as a Risk Mitigator: As discussed earlier, insurance plays a vital role in managing risk. Having adequate coverage for health, life, home, auto, and other risks provides protection and financial support when unforeseen events occur.

Regular Reviews: Periodically review your financial plan and insurance coverage to ensure they remain in line with your current circumstances and goals. Life events, such as marriage, having children, or retirement, may necessitate adjustments to your risk management strategy.

Risk Tolerance and Time Horizon: Assessing your risk tolerance and investment time horizon are vital when making financial decisions. Understanding how much risk you can comfortably handle and the length of time you can invest before needing the funds guides your risk management choices.

Long-Term Perspective: Maintaining a long-term perspective is essential for navigating financial risks.

Avoid making impulsive decisions based on short-term market fluctuations, as they may lead to losses or missed opportunities.

Seeking Professional Advice: Consulting with a financial advisor can provide valuable insights into identifying and managing risks effectively. A professional can help tailor a risk management strategy to suit your individual circumstances and goals.

Mental and Emotional Preparedness: Being mentally prepared for the possibility of risks materializing can help you respond rationally to unforeseen events. Staying disciplined and emotionally balanced during turbulent times can prevent hasty decisions that may harm your financial objectives.

Understanding and managing risk effectively is a fundamental pillar of a comprehensive financial plan. By proactively identifying potential risks, implementing strategic risk management strategies, and remaining adaptable to changing circumstances, you can protect your financial future and confidently pursue your long-term goals. A well-structured approach to risk management, coupled with adequate insurance coverage, provides you with the resilience and flexibility needed to navigate life's uncertainties with confidence.

Chapter 10: Your Wealth Preservation & Financial Education

As you journey towards financial prosperity, it becomes vital to equip yourself with the knowledge and strategies necessary to not only grow your wealth but also preserve it for future generations. In this chapter, we will delve into the dynamic realm of wealth preservation and financial education, exploring prudent approaches that will safeguard your hard-earned assets and empower you to make informed financial decisions. By embracing the principles outlined herein, you can lay the groundwork for a lasting legacy that transcends time and empowers you to contribute to causes that hold personal significance. Let us embark on this enlightening voyage, where the horizon is boundless, and the rewards are immeasurable.

• *Strategies for Preserving and Growing Wealth:*

Diversification: The Time-Tested Shield

The adage "don't put all your eggs in one basket" resonates profoundly in the realm of wealth preservation. Diversifying your investments across various asset classes, such as stocks, bonds, real estate, and commodities, mitigates risk and shields your portfolio from potential downturns in specific sectors. A well-balanced and diversified portfolio can weather economic storms and provide consistent returns over the long term, reinforcing the foundation of your financial security.

The Power of Compound Interest: Start Early, Benefit Forever

Albert Einstein famously referred to compound interest as the "eighth wonder of the world." Indeed, harnessing the magic of compounding can significantly accelerate your wealth growth. By starting early and consistently contributing to investment vehicles like retirement accounts and tax-advantaged savings plans, you can witness your wealth grow exponentially over time. Embracing patience and discipline in this pursuit ensures the rewards of compound interest become an enduring force in your financial journey.

Estate Planning: Securing Your Legacy

Crafting a comprehensive estate plan is not solely an exercise in navigating legal intricacies; it is an act of love and consideration for those you hold dear. Carefully thought-out wills, trusts, and other estate planning tools can safeguard your assets and ensure they are distributed according to your wishes. Moreover, estate planning can mitigate tax liabilities, leaving more of your hard-earned wealth to benefit your heirs and cherished causes.

Philanthropy: Leaving a Lasting Impact

As you amass wealth and cultivate financial success, consider the transformative power of philanthropy. Giving back to society allows you to support charitable organizations and causes that align with your values, leaving a positive and lasting impact on communities and future generations. Embracing a philanthropic approach not only enriches the lives of others but also provides personal fulfillment and a sense of purpose in your financial journey.

Continual Financial Education: Empowering Your Wealth Strategy

The world of finance is dynamic, shaped by ever-changing economic landscapes and evolving investment opportunities. To navigate this complexity, commit yourself to lifelong financial education. Stay informed about market trends, emerging technologies, and innovative financial tools. Continuously improving your financial literacy empowers you to make informed decisions, adapt to changing circumstances, and identify lucrative opportunities that contribute to your long-term financial well-being.

As you integrate these strategies into your financial blueprint, you pave the way for enduring prosperity and a legacy that extends far beyond your lifetime. By preserving and growing your wealth thoughtfully, you secure not only your own financial future but also the futures of those you hold dear and the causes that ignite your passion. Embrace the power of knowledge and strategic planning, and embark on a journey where financial abundance and meaningful impact converge harmoniously.

• *Estate Planning and Asset Protection:*

Estate Planning: Crafting Your Legacy

Estate planning is not just about distributing your wealth; it is a profound act of love and consideration for your loved ones and cherished causes. Work with a qualified estate planning attorney to create a comprehensive plan that reflects your wishes and values. A well-crafted will ensures that your assets are distributed according to your desires, while trusts offer additional benefits such as privacy, probate avoidance, and control over the timing and manner of distribution. Review and update your estate plan regularly to accommodate life changes and ensure its continued relevance.

Asset Protection: Safeguarding Your Wealth

As you build and preserve your wealth, safeguarding it from potential threats becomes paramount. Asset protection involves structuring your financial affairs to shield your assets from creditors, legal claims, or other risks. Asset protection strategies may include the use of trusts, limited liability entities, and insurance policies. By proactively protecting your assets, you can shield your wealth from unforeseen circumstances, enhancing your financial security and peace of mind.

Charitable Giving and Philanthropy: Impactful Contributions

Embracing philanthropy not only benefits society but also offers various tax advantages and estate planning benefits. Engage in charitable giving by supporting causes that resonate with you, whether through direct donations, charitable trusts, donor-advised funds, or establishing a foundation. Consult with your financial advisor to optimize the tax efficiency of your charitable contributions, enabling you to make a more significant impact while maximizing your wealth preservation goals.

Legacy Planning: Passing on Your Values

Your legacy extends beyond material possessions; it encompasses the values and principles you hold dear. Consider creating a legacy plan that outlines your beliefs, stories, and life lessons for future generations. This intangible inheritance can strengthen family bonds and perpetuate the guiding principles that have shaped your success. A well-crafted legacy plan ensures that your values endure as an enduring reflection of your life's journey.

Privacy and Identity Protection: A Digital Age Concern

In today's digital age, safeguarding your personal information and digital assets is critical. Review your online accounts, passwords, and digital estate plan to protect your identity and ensure a smooth transition of digital assets in the event of your incapacity or passing. Including a digital executor in your estate plan can help manage and distribute your digital assets according to your wishes.

Business Succession Planning: Perpetuating Your Vision

If you are a business owner, proper succession planning is vital to preserve the legacy of your company. Identify potential successors, develop a clear succession plan, and outline the transfer of ownership and responsibilities. Business succession planning ensures a seamless transition, minimizes disruptions, and secures the longevity of your entrepreneurial vision.

Periodic Review and Revision: Adapting to Change

Life is dynamic, and your financial circumstances will evolve over time. Regularly review your estate plan and asset protection strategies to reflect changes in your family structure, financial goals, and legal regulations. A well-maintained estate plan ensures that your wishes are continually upheld, and your wealth preservation goals remain on track.

Seeking Professional Guidance: Expert Advice Matters

Estate planning and asset protection are complex endeavors that require specialized knowledge. Enlist the services of an experienced estate planning attorney and financial advisor who can collaborate to devise a comprehensive plan tailored to your unique needs. Their guidance ensures that your estate plan aligns with your long-term objectives and stands strong against legal complexities.

State planning and asset protection form the bedrock of securing your financial legacy and providing for your loved ones in the future. By crafting a well-considered estate plan and implementing effective asset protection strategies, you establish a solid framework for preserving your wealth and leaving a lasting impact on the people and causes that matter most to you. Embrace these essential components of financial planning with care and diligence, knowing that they are the cornerstones of a prosperous and enduring legacy.

• *Exploring Trusts and Wills:*

Wills: A Time-Honored Foundation

A last will and testament are the cornerstone of any comprehensive estate plan. A will allows you to specify how you wish to distribute your assets after your passing, appoint guardians for minor children, and designate an executor to oversee the administration of your estate. Without a valid will, your estate may be subject to intestate laws, potentially leading to unintended consequences and delays in asset distribution. Work with a knowledgeable estate planning attorney to draft a will that accurately reflects your wishes, providing clarity and certainty to your loved ones during a challenging time.

Revocable Living Trust: Maintaining Control and Privacy

A revocable living trust is an essential tool for estate planning, providing numerous benefits during your lifetime and after. By transferring assets into the trust, you maintain control over them while avoiding probate upon your passing. This privacy-enhancing approach allows your beneficiaries to avoid the public scrutiny and costly court proceedings associated with probate. A living trust also permits the seamless management of your affairs if you become incapacitated, ensuring that your financial matters are handled according to your preferences.

Irrevocable Trusts: Asset Protection and Tax Efficiency

Irrevocable trusts serve as potent vehicles for asset protection and tax planning. By transferring assets into an irrevocable trust, you remove them from your estate, potentially reducing estate tax liabilities and protecting them from creditors. Irrevocable trusts can also facilitate Medicaid planning, enabling you to preserve assets while qualifying for government assistance for long-term care if necessary. Careful consideration and professional advice are vital when implementing an irrevocable trust, as its terms are unalterable once established.

Testamentary Trusts: Providing for Loved Ones

A testamentary trust is created within your will and takes effect upon your passing. This type of trust allows you to allocate assets for specific beneficiaries while retaining control over your estate during your lifetime. Testamentary trusts are commonly used to support minor children or beneficiaries with special needs, ensuring that their inheritances are managed responsibly by a designated trustee until they reach a specified age or milestone.

Special Needs Trusts: Securing Future Care

For individuals with special needs or disabilities, a special needs trust provides a crucial means of preserving eligibility for government benefits while supplementing care and quality of life. Funds held in a properly structured special needs trust do not count as assets for means-tested programs, allowing beneficiaries to access crucial government assistance without compromising their inheritance. Designing a special needs trust requires careful attention to complex regulations, making professional guidance indispensable.

Charitable Trusts: Giving with Purpose

Charitable trusts allow you to support charitable organizations while potentially receiving tax benefits and preserving your wealth. Charitable remainder trusts offer income for the donor or beneficiaries during their lifetimes, with the remaining assets ultimately benefiting the chosen charity. Charitable lead trusts, on the other hand, provide annual payments to the charitable organization for a specified period, after which the remaining assets return to the donor or their designated beneficiaries. Implementing charitable trusts allows you to leave a legacy of philanthropy while maximizing the impact of your charitable contributions.

Dynasty Trusts: Enduring Legacy

A dynasty trust is designed to span multiple generations, preserving your wealth and legacy for your descendants while minimizing estate taxes. By establishing a dynasty trust, you can transfer substantial assets to future generations without triggering estate tax liabilities at each transfer. This powerful tool enables you to create a lasting financial legacy that provides for your family's well-being and aspirations for years to come.

Family Limited Partnerships: Unified Wealth Management

Family limited partnerships (FLPs) facilitate seamless wealth transfer within a family and offer tax benefits while allowing for centralized management of family assets. By consolidating family assets into the FLP, you can maintain control while gifting limited partnership interests to family members, reducing estate tax exposure, and protecting assets from potential creditors. Consult with legal and financial experts to structure an FLP that aligns with your family's unique dynamics and financial goals.

Exploring trusts and wills unlocks an array of powerful estate planning tools that can secure your assets, provide for your loved ones, and make a meaningful impact on the causes you hold dear. By carefully crafting a comprehensive estate plan that incorporates these instruments, you take control of your financial legacy, ensuring that your wealth endures for generations and contributes to the betterment of society. Embrace the potential of trusts and wills as integral components of your estate planning journey, allowing you to navigate the complexities of wealth preservation with confidence and compassion.

• *Charitable Giving and Philanthropy:*

Charitable Giving: The Joy of Impactful Contributions

Embracing charitable giving goes beyond financial transactions; it reflects a deep desire to create positive change in the world. Cultivating a giving mindset and making a meaningful impact on causes you are passionate about brings immense fulfillment. As you contemplate your charitable endeavors, consider the causes that resonate with your values and align with your financial capacity. From supporting local community initiatives to championing global causes, your contributions can make a significant difference in the lives of others.

Donor-Advised Funds: A Flexible Giving Solution

Donor-advised funds (DAFs) offer a flexible and streamlined approach to charitable giving. Establishing a DAF allows you to make a tax-deductible contribution and receive an immediate charitable deduction, even if you have not yet decided on specific charitable recipients. Over time, you can recommend grants from the fund to the charities of your choice, enabling you to carefully consider the impact and effectiveness of your philanthropic contributions.

Impact Investing: Aligning Values with Returns

As the realm of philanthropy evolves, impact investing emerges as a powerful tool that unites financial goals with social and environmental causes. Impact investing involves allocating capital to businesses, projects, and initiatives that generate positive social and environmental outcomes while also delivering financial returns. By embracing impact investing, you contribute to causes that align with your values, effectively leveraging your financial resources to drive lasting change in society.

Creating a Family Philanthropy Plan: Uniting Generations

Philanthropy can be a catalyst for family unity and instilling shared values across generations. Establishing a family philanthropy plan involves involving family members in charitable discussions, decision-making, and giving. Engage in open conversations about the causes that matter to each family member and collaboratively identify charitable initiatives that reflect the collective values of the family. Family philanthropy strengthens bonds and creates a lasting legacy of compassion and empathy for future generations.

Structuring Charitable Gifts: Optimizing Tax Benefits

Strategically structuring charitable gifts can maximize their impact while providing attractive tax benefits. By donating appreciated assets such as stocks or real estate directly to charitable organizations, you can avoid capital gains tax and potentially claim a charitable deduction for the fair market value of the donated assets. Leveraging philanthropy with tax planning enables you to magnify the value of your contributions and support causes more effectively.

Planned Giving: Leave a Legacy

Planned giving allows you to contribute to charitable organizations during your lifetime while creating a lasting legacy for the future. Various planned giving vehicles, such as charitable remainder trusts or charitable lead trusts, can be employed to support charitable initiatives while providing income for you or your beneficiaries. Discussing planned giving options with your financial advisor and estate planning attorney enables you to structure gifts that align with your financial goals and philanthropic aspirations.

Corporate Social Responsibility: Business as a Force for Good

If you are a business owner or executive, incorporating corporate social responsibility (CSR)

into your company's culture can generate positive impact and goodwill. Integrating philanthropic initiatives into your business strategy, such as charitable donations, employee volunteer programs, or sustainable business practices, not only benefits society but also strengthens your brand and fosters employee engagement.

Measuring Impact: The Journey of Change

As you engage in charitable giving and philanthropy, measuring the impact of your contributions becomes crucial. By evaluating the outcomes and effectiveness of charitable initiatives, you can refine your giving strategy and enhance the impact of your philanthropic endeavors. Partnering with reputable organizations and conducting due diligence ensures that your donations are channeled efficiently to create sustainable change.

Charitable giving and philanthropy represent a powerful means of expressing compassion and shaping a better world. By integrating philanthropic initiatives into your financial plan and embracing the joy of giving, you can make a lasting impact on the causes you cherish. Whether through traditional donations, impact investing, or family-focused philanthropy, your contributions serve as a beacon of hope and create a legacy of compassion that transcends time. Embrace the transformative potential of charitable giving and philanthropy as a driving force for positive change, leaving an enduring imprint on the world and the lives of those less fortunate.

• *The Importance of Ongoing Financial Education:*

Lifelong Learning: The Cornerstone of Financial Mastery

In the ever-evolving landscape of personal finance, the importance of ongoing financial education cannot be overstated. Just as the world of investments, taxes, and economic trends continues to change, so too must your understanding of these concepts. Committing to a journey of lifelong learning empowers you to stay informed, adapt to shifting circumstances, and make well-informed financial decisions that align with your goals.

Building Financial Confidence: Empowerment through Knowledge

Financial education is more than just learning about numbers and formulas; it is about building the confidence to navigate complex financial decisions with clarity and purpose. The more you understand various financial concepts, the more in control you feel about your financial future. Armed with knowledge, you can approach financial challenges with confidence, making choices that resonate with your values and promote long-term prosperity.

Expanding Investment Horizons: Embracing New Opportunities

As financial markets evolve, so do investment opportunities. Ongoing financial education exposes you to new investment strategies and emerging asset classes, enabling you to diversify your portfolio and seek potentially higher returns. By staying abreast of investment trends, you can make well-informed decisions that align with your risk tolerance and financial objectives.

Navigating Tax Complexity: Maximizing Efficiency

Tax laws are subject to change, and navigating the intricacies of taxation requires continual education. Staying updated on tax regulations empowers you to capitalize on tax-saving opportunities and optimize your financial plan. By understanding the tax implications of various financial decisions, you can minimize tax liabilities and retain more of your hard-earned wealth.

Adapting to Economic Trends: Seizing Opportunities

Economic landscapes can shift dramatically over time, impacting everything from interest rates to employment opportunities. Ongoing financial education equips you to recognize economic trends and adapt your financial strategies accordingly. By staying ahead of economic developments, you can position yourself to capitalize on opportunities and mitigate potential risks.

Reinforcing Budgeting and Saving Habits: Maintaining Discipline

A key aspect of financial success lies in maintaining disciplined budgeting and saving habits. Ongoing financial education reinforces the importance of prudent money management and the benefits of consistent saving. Through continuous learning, you can discover new techniques to optimize your budget, increase your savings rate, and accelerate your progress towards financial goals.

Nurturing Resilience: Overcoming Challenges

Life is rife with unforeseen challenges, and financial setbacks can occur at any time. A strong foundation of financial education instills resilience, enabling you to navigate through tough times and bounce back from setbacks. By understanding risk management and contingency planning, you can face uncertainties with composure, knowing that you have the knowledge and tools to recover and rebuild.

Informed Decision-Making: Minimizing Costly Mistakes

Financial decisions often carry significant consequences, both in the short and long term. Ongoing financial education minimizes the likelihood of making costly mistakes, such as impulsive investments, inadequate insurance coverage, or misaligned estate planning. By basing decisions on knowledge and informed analysis, you can sidestep pitfalls and optimize outcomes.

Enhancing Financial Wellness: A Journey of Well-Being

At its core, financial education contributes to overall financial wellness and peace of mind. By fostering a holistic understanding of personal finance, you create a harmonious relationship with money, one that transcends mere numbers and becomes a reflection of your values and aspirations. As you cultivate financial well-being, you lay the groundwork for a fulfilling life that encompasses not only monetary success but also emotional security and purpose.

The journey of ongoing financial education is a transformative one, equipping you with the knowledge and skills to thrive in an ever-changing financial landscape. As you embrace lifelong learning, you nurture financial confidence, expand your investment horizons, and adapt to economic shifts. Through continuous education, you empower yourself to make well-informed decisions, strengthen your financial resilience, and achieve lasting prosperity and well-being. Embrace the profound impact of ongoing financial education as a guiding light, illuminating the path to financial freedom and enriching every aspect of your life.

• *Resources for Expanding Financial Knowledge:*

Books: The Timeless Wisdom of Literature

Books remain an invaluable resource for expanding financial knowledge. From classic finance and investing texts to contemporary personal finance guides, books offer in-depth insights and diverse perspectives on various financial topics. Look for acclaimed authors and well-reviewed titles that cater to your specific interests and learning objectives. The wealth of knowledge found within the pages of books can inspire and enlighten, paving the way for a deeper understanding of financial principles and strategies.

Online Courses: Learning at Your Fingertips

The digital era has brought a wealth of financial education opportunities directly to your fingertips. Numerous reputable platforms offer online courses on finance, investing, budgeting, and more. These courses often include interactive lessons, quizzes, and expert guidance to ensure a comprehensive learning experience. Whether you are a beginner seeking foundational knowledge or a seasoned investor looking to refine your skills, online courses provide flexibility and convenience in your pursuit of financial education.

Webinars and Podcasts: Insights from Experts

Webinars and podcasts have emerged as dynamic mediums for sharing financial knowledge. Experts and industry professionals host these engaging sessions, offering insights on current financial trends, investment strategies, and practical money management tips. Subscribing to reputable financial podcasts or attending webinars conducted by renowned financial gurus can keep you updated on the latest developments in the financial world and expand your expertise.

Financial News Outlets: Stay Informed

Keeping abreast of financial news is crucial for staying informed about market trends and economic developments. Trusted financial news outlets, both in print and digital formats, provide real-time updates on global markets, business news, and financial regulations. Regularly consuming financial news enriches your understanding of the factors influencing the economy and your investments, enabling you to make informed decisions.

Personal Finance Blogs: Insights from Peers

Personal finance blogs are a treasure trove of insights, tips, and real-life experiences shared by financial bloggers and enthusiasts. Reading personal finance blogs offers a relatable perspective on money management, investment strategies, and overcoming financial challenges. Engage with blog communities to exchange ideas, seek advice, and learn from the experiences of others on their financial journeys.

Financial Advisors: Expert Guidance

Financial advisors play a pivotal role in expanding financial knowledge by providing personalized guidance and strategic planning. Engaging a qualified financial advisor offers access to expert insights and tailored financial strategies aligned with your unique goals. Regular consultations with your advisor enable you to address questions, explore new opportunities, and continuously refine your financial plan.

Community Seminars and Workshops: Collaborative Learning

Many communities host financial seminars and workshops where local experts share their knowledge with attendees. These events foster collaborative learning environments and allow you to interact with financial professionals and like-minded individuals. Participating in community-based financial events can enhance your financial knowledge while strengthening your network of peers with similar interests.

Online Forums and Discussion Groups: Sharing and Learning Together

Joining online forums and discussion groups dedicated to personal finance enables you to connect with a diverse community of individuals seeking to expand their financial knowledge. Engage in discussions, seek advice, and share insights with others who share your passion for financial learning. Active participation in such forums fosters continuous learning and offers support on your financial journey.

Financial Literacy Organizations: Advocating for Education

Several reputable organizations are dedicated to promoting financial literacy and education. These organizations offer free resources, educational programs, and tools to help individuals enhance their financial acumen. Connecting with financial literacy organizations and accessing their resources can further enrich your financial knowledge and empower you to make informed decisions.

University and College Courses: Formal Education

Universities and colleges offer formal courses in finance, economics, and business that provide in-depth knowledge and recognized qualifications. Enrolling in finance-related courses can lay a strong academic foundation for a career in finance or enhance your understanding of complex financial concepts. Many institutions offer both traditional and online options, providing flexibility to fit learning into your schedule.

Resources for expanding financial knowledge are abundant and diverse, catering to individuals with varying learning preferences and goals. From books and online courses to podcasts, financial advisors, and community events, each resource contributes uniquely to your financial education journey. Embrace the wealth of opportunities available to enrich your financial knowledge and approach your ongoing financial education with enthusiasm and dedication. Empower yourself with the tools and insights needed to achieve financial success, navigate financial challenges, and cultivate lasting prosperity in every aspect of your life.

• *Understanding Economic Trends and Market Forces:*

Economic Indicators: Insights into the Economy

Economic indicators serve as vital signposts that offer insights into the health and direction of the economy. Monitoring key indicators, such as gross domestic product (GDP), inflation rates, employment data, and consumer confidence, enables you to understand economic trends and anticipate potential shifts. By keeping a close eye on economic indicators, you can make informed financial decisions, adjust your investment strategy, and position yourself to capitalize on emerging opportunities.

Market Analysis: Unveiling Investment Potential

Thorough market analysis is essential for investors seeking to navigate the dynamic world of financial markets. Understanding market forces that drive asset prices, such as supply and demand, geopolitical events, and central bank policies, empowers you to assess investment risks and opportunities more effectively. Engaging in comprehensive market research and staying informed about market sentiment allows you to make prudent investment choices aligned with your financial goals.

Sector and Industry Performance: Identifying Growth Areas

The performance of different sectors and industries can vary significantly based on economic conditions and market forces. Analyzing sector performance provides valuable insights into areas of growth and potential investment opportunities. By diversifying your portfolio across various sectors, you can take advantage of the strengths of different industries while mitigating risks associated with sector-specific challenges.

Technological Advancements: The Disruptive Impact

The rapidly evolving landscape of technology has a profound impact on the economy and financial markets. Technological advancements, such as artificial intelligence, blockchain, and renewable energy solutions, create both opportunities and disruptions across industries. Understanding the implications of technological trends allows you to identify potential investment prospects and adapt your financial strategies to stay ahead in the ever-changing economic landscape.

Global Events and Geopolitics: Shaping Economic Realities

Global events and geopolitical developments exert significant influence on economic trends and market movements. Factors such as trade agreements, political stability, and international conflicts can impact economies and financial markets on a global scale. Staying informed about global events and their potential consequences enables you to adjust your financial approach and navigate uncertain economic waters with resilience.

Interest Rates and Monetary Policy: Impact on Investments

Central banks' monetary policies, including interest rate decisions and quantitative easing measures, have far-reaching implications for investors. Changes in interest rates can influence borrowing costs, consumer spending, and asset valuations. Understanding the interplay between monetary policy and financial markets allows you to adjust your investment strategy based on prevailing interest rate environments.

Behavioral Finance: Emotions and Investment Decisions

Behavioral finance examines the psychological factors that influence investment decisions. Understanding common behavioral biases, such as loss aversion and herd mentality, helps you recognize and mitigate emotional biases that may cloud your judgment. Cultivating self-awareness and making investment decisions based on rational analysis rather than emotions contribute to more disciplined and successful investing.

Economic Cycles: Preparing for Ups and Downs

The economy operates in cycles of expansion, contraction, and recovery. Familiarizing yourself with economic cycles equips you to anticipate potential changes in financial markets and adjust your investment strategy accordingly. By diversifying your investments across different asset classes, you can better weather economic downturns and capitalize on growth opportunities during economic upswings.

Risk Management in Uncertain Times: Preserving Capital

Understanding economic trends and market forces is essential for effective risk management. During times of economic uncertainty, it is crucial to assess your risk tolerance, review your portfolio, and consider defensive strategies to preserve capital.

Diversification, asset allocation, and periodic rebalancing are fundamental risk management tools that help you maintain financial stability through market fluctuations.

Long-Term Perspective: Patience in Investing

While economic trends and market forces can be volatile in the short term, maintaining a long-term perspective is crucial for successful investing. Avoiding knee-jerk reactions to market fluctuations and staying committed to your financial plan can lead to more consistent and favorable outcomes over time.

Understanding economic trends and market forces is an essential aspect of financial literacy. Equipped with knowledge about economic indicators, market analysis, and global events, you can make informed financial decisions and adapt your strategies to capitalize on opportunities while mitigating risks. Embrace the continuous learning journey of understanding economic trends and market forces, as it is a cornerstone of successful investing and financial planning. By combining knowledge and discipline, you position yourself for enduring financial prosperity and resilience in the ever-changing landscape of finance and economics.

• Continuously Improving Your Financial Literacy:

Embracing Lifelong Learning: A Commitment to Growth

Financial literacy is not a destination but a lifelong journey of growth and self-improvement. Embrace the mindset of continuous learning, as the world of finance and economics is ever-changing. Commit to expanding your financial knowledge through reading, attending seminars, participating in webinars, and engaging in discussions with experts and peers. The more you invest in your financial education, the better equipped you become to navigate complexities, make informed decisions, and achieve long-term financial success.

Setting Learning Goals: Charting Your Path

Just as you set financial goals, establish learning goals that align with your evolving interests and financial aspirations. Identify specific areas of finance you wish to explore, such as investment strategies, retirement planning, or tax optimization. By setting learning goals, you create a roadmap for your financial education journey and remain focused on acquiring the knowledge and skills you need to achieve your objectives.

Seeking Mentorship: Learning from Experience

Mentorship plays a pivotal role in honing your financial literacy. Seek out mentors who possess expertise in areas you wish to master, whether it's investing, entrepreneurship, or personal finance. Mentors can offer valuable insights, guidance, and real-life experiences that complement your formal education and enrich your understanding of financial concepts and strategies.

Participating in Workshops and Seminars: Immersive Experiences

Workshops and seminars provide immersive learning experiences, allowing you to delve deeper into specific financial topics and interact with experts in the field. Look for workshops that cater to your interests and learning style, and take advantage of these opportunities to gain practical knowledge and network with like-minded individuals.

Financial Simulations and Games: Learning through Play

Engaging in financial simulations and games offers a fun and interactive approach to learning. Many online platforms offer simulations that allow you to experiment with investment strategies and experience the impact of financial decisions in a risk-free environment. These games foster a deeper understanding of financial concepts and provide valuable lessons in a playful and engaging manner.

Joining Investment Clubs: Collaborative Learning

Investment clubs are groups of individuals who come together to study and invest in financial markets collectively. Joining an investment club fosters collaborative learning and provides a forum for discussing investment ideas and strategies with fellow members. The diversity of perspectives in an investment club enriches your financial knowledge and helps you refine your investment approach.

Reflecting on Financial Decisions: Learning from Mistakes

Self-reflection is a powerful tool for improving financial literacy. Regularly review your financial decisions, both successful and unsuccessful, to understand the factors that influenced your choices. By learning from past mistakes and successes, you can fine-tune your decision-making process and become a more discerning and informed financial manager.

Attending Financial Conferences: Industry Insights

Financial conferences bring together experts and thought leaders from various sectors of the finance industry. These events offer unique opportunities to hear firsthand insights, trends, and predictions about financial markets, investments, and economic developments. Attending financial conferences broadens your perspective and keeps you abreast of the latest trends and innovations in finance.

Educating Family Members: Empowering Generations

Sharing your financial knowledge with family members, especially children, cultivates a culture of financial literacy and empowerment. Educating younger generations about money management, saving, and investing instills valuable life skills that contribute to their long-term financial well-being. Engaging in financial discussions as a family, fosters open communication and creates a support system for mutual learning and growth.

Contributing to Financial Literacy Initiatives: Paying It Forward

As you continuously improve your financial literacy, consider giving back to the community by supporting financial literacy initiatives. Volunteer with organizations that promote financial education in schools or underserved communities. By sharing your knowledge and experiences, you become a catalyst for positive change, empowering others to take control of their financial futures.

Continuously improving your financial literacy is a transformative journey that fuels personal growth, confidence, and financial success. By embracing lifelong learning, setting learning goals, seeking mentorship, and participating in immersive experiences, you equip yourself with the knowledge and skills to make informed financial decisions. Reflect on your financial choices, engage in collaborative learning, and contribute to financial literacy initiatives to empower yourself and others. Embrace the adventure of continuous improvement, knowing that each step you take brings you closer to mastering the art of financial management and securing a brighter future.

Chapter 11: Your Financial Freedom

In this chapter, we embark on a journey to explore the concept of financial freedom – a state of being that many dream of but often struggle to attain. Financial freedom goes beyond mere monetary wealth; it represents the liberation from financial stress and the ability to live life on your terms, pursuing your passions and aspirations without being constrained by financial limitations. Throughout this chapter, we will delve into the core essence of financial freedom, understand what it truly means for you, and outline the transformative steps you can take to attain this coveted state of abundance.

• *Defining Financial Freedom*

Financial freedom is a state of financial well-being and independence that grants you the freedom to make choices that align with your values, goals, and desires, unburdened by financial constraints. It is not about achieving opulence or unbridled luxury; instead, it revolves around the empowerment that comes from having a solid financial foundation, one that provides you with the means to lead a fulfilling and purpose-driven life.

At its essence, financial freedom offers you the following key attributes:

Peace of Mind: With financial freedom, you can experience peace of mind, knowing that you have the resources to handle unexpected challenges and emergencies without derailing your long-term financial goals. The elimination of financial stress allows you to focus on what truly matters to you — family, personal growth, and contributing to society.

Choice and Flexibility: Achieving financial freedom bestows the freedom of choice. It enables you to make decisions without being forced into unfavorable options due to financial constraints. Whether it's choosing a career path you're passionate about, taking time off to travel, or pursuing further education, you have the flexibility to shape your life as you see fit.

Pursuit of Passion: Financial freedom liberates you to pursue your passions and interests, without the worry of financial repercussions. You can dedicate time and resources to hobbies, projects, or charitable causes that ignite your soul, enhancing your overall well-being and sense of fulfillment.

Reduced Stress and Enhanced Relationships: Sound financial footing brings harmony to your personal relationships. Financial worries often strain partnerships, family ties, and friendships. By achieving financial freedom, you can strengthen these bonds and nurture a more joyful and supportive environment.

Generosity and Impact: Beyond personal benefits, financial freedom allows you to impact the lives of others positively. With the capacity to contribute to charitable endeavors or support causes close to your heart, you can leave a meaningful legacy and create a ripple effect of positive change in the world.

As we delve deeper into this chapter, we will explore the practical strategies and mindset shifts necessary to achieve financial freedom. From understanding your unique vision of financial freedom to implementing intentional actions, you will be empowered to take significant steps towards unlocking your true potential and embracing a life of abundance, purpose, and contentment. So, let us embark on this transformative journey together, and unlock the doors to your financial freedom.

• *Steps to Achieve Financial Freedom*

Step 1: Set Clear Financial Goals

The first crucial step towards achieving financial freedom is to set clear and realistic financial goals. Take the time to envision your ideal life and define what financial freedom means to you. Consider both short-term and long-term objectives, such as paying off debt, building an emergency fund, buying a home, funding your children's education, and retiring comfortably. Establishing these goals will provide a clear roadmap for your financial journey and serve as a source of motivation throughout the process.

Step 2: Assess Your Current Financial Situation

To effectively chart your path towards financial freedom, it is essential to have a comprehensive understanding of your current financial situation. Create a detailed inventory of your assets, liabilities, income sources, and expenses. Evaluate your spending patterns, identify areas where you can cut back, and redirect those savings towards your financial goals. This assessment will help you determine where you stand financially and allow you to make informed decisions moving forward.

Step 3: Build a Solid Budget

Developing a well-structured budget is a fundamental aspect of achieving financial freedom. Use the insights gained from your financial assessment to create a budget that aligns with your goals. Categorize your expenses, distinguishing between essential needs and discretionary spending. Strive to live below your means, ensuring that you have surplus funds to allocate towards savings and investments. A well-managed budget empowers you to take control of your finances and make progress towards your financial freedom milestones.

Step 4: Eliminate Debt Strategically

Debt can be a significant obstacle on the path to financial freedom. Devise a strategic plan to tackle your debts effectively. Prioritize high-interest debts and work towards paying them off first. Employ debt repayment strategies such as the snowball method or the avalanche method, depending on your preferences and circumstances. As you gradually reduce your debt burden, you will free up more resources to accelerate your progress towards financial independence.

Step 5: Build an Emergency Fund

An emergency fund acts as a safety net during unforeseen circumstances, providing financial stability and preventing setbacks on your journey to financial freedom. Aim to save three to six months' worth of living expenses in a readily accessible account. This fund will shield you from dipping into your investments or going into debt when unexpected expenses arise, allowing you to stay on track with your long-term financial objectives.

Step 6: Invest Wisely and Diversify

Investing wisely is a critical component of wealth accumulation and long-term financial freedom. Educate yourself on various investment options, such as stocks, bonds, real estate, and mutual funds. Diversify your investment portfolio to spread risk and maximize potential returns. Consider seeking advice from a qualified financial advisor who can help tailor an investment strategy that aligns with your risk tolerance and financial goals.

Step 7: Maximize Retirement Savings

Planning for retirement is essential to ensure a comfortable and worry-free future. Take advantage of retirement accounts, such as 401(k)s or Individual Retirement Accounts (IRAs), and contribute consistently to benefit from compound interest and potential employer matches. Start saving for retirement early to harness the power of time and enable your investments to grow steadily over the years.

Step 8: Continuously Educate Yourself

Financial knowledge is a valuable asset on your journey to financial freedom. Commit to continuous education about personal finance, investment strategies, and economic trends. Stay informed about changes in tax laws, financial regulations, and market dynamics. A strong financial education will empower you to make informed decisions, adapt to changing circumstances, and optimize your path to financial freedom.

Step 9: Stay Disciplined and Persistent

The path to financial freedom may present challenges and require discipline and perseverance. Stay committed to your goals, maintaining the discipline to follow your budget, and stick to your financial plan. Celebrate milestones and progress, no matter how small, and use setbacks as learning opportunities. Remember that financial freedom is a journey, and staying persistent will lead you to greater achievements over time.

Step 10: Enjoy the Fruits of Financial Freedom

As you approach financial freedom, take the time to enjoy the fruits of your labor. Embrace the newfound flexibility and choices that financial independence provides. Use your resources to support causes you are passionate about, indulge in experiences that bring you joy, and share your success with loved ones. Appreciate the journey you have undertaken and savor the freedom that comes with financial security.

Achieving financial freedom is a transformative and rewarding process that requires careful planning, dedication, and perseverance. By setting clear goals, adopting prudent financial habits, and investing wisely, you can unlock the door to financial freedom and live a life of abundance and purpose. Remember, every step you take towards financial independence is a step closer to realizing your dreams and aspirations. Embrace the power of financial knowledge and discipline, and embark on your journey towards a future of true financial freedom.

• *Enjoying the Benefits of Financial Freedom*

As you reach the pinnacle of financial freedom, you enter a phase of life where the true rewards of your efforts come to fruition. Embracing the benefits that financial independence offers, you can experience a profound and positive shift in various aspects of your life. Let's explore the many ways in which financial freedom enhances your overall well-being and allows you to savor a life of abundance and contentment.

Pursuing Passions and Dreams: Financial freedom opens the door to pursuing your passions and dreams without constraints. Whether it's starting your own business, traveling the world, or engaging in creative endeavors, you have the autonomy to turn your aspirations into reality. Your newfound financial flexibility empowers you to invest time and resources in activities that bring you joy and fulfillment.

Embracing Minimalism and Conscious Spending: With the freedom from financial pressures, you may find yourself adopting a more mindful approach to spending. Financially secure individuals often appreciate the value of experiences over material possessions. Embracing minimalism allows you to focus on meaningful connections, experiences, and personal growth, leading to a more fulfilling and balanced life.

Supporting Loved Ones and Giving Back: Financial freedom enables you to support your loved ones and contribute to causes close to your heart. Whether it's providing for your family, funding your children's education, or supporting charitable organizations, your ability to give back creates a positive impact on the lives of others and fosters a sense of purpose.

Redefining Work-Life Balance: Achieving financial freedom allows you to redefine your work-life balance. You have the option to pursue work that aligns with your passions and interests, rather than being solely motivated by financial necessities. This newfound balance promotes overall well-being and enhances job satisfaction.

Building a Lasting Legacy: With financial independence comes the opportunity to leave a lasting legacy for future generations. You can plan and allocate resources to ensure that your loved ones are financially secure and supported even after you're gone. Establishing trusts, endowments, or contributing to charitable foundations allows you to create a positive impact that extends beyond your lifetime.

Fostering Peace of Mind: Financial freedom provides a profound sense of peace and security. You are better equipped to handle unforeseen challenges, emergencies, or economic downturns without fear of financial ruin. This peace of mind allows you to enjoy life's precious moments and focus on personal growth and self-improvement.

Expanding Your Horizons: Financial freedom opens up a world of opportunities. Whether it's exploring new hobbies, pursuing further education, or engaging in cultural experiences, you have the freedom to broaden your horizons and continually evolve as an individual.

Building Strong Relationships: The freedom from financial stress often leads to improved personal relationships. Financially secure individuals can focus on building stronger connections with their loved ones, unburdened by money-related worries. These strengthened relationships become a source of emotional support and fulfillment.

Leveraging Generational Wealth: By strategically preserving and growing your wealth, you can leverage generational wealth that benefits your descendants for years to come. Passing down financial knowledge and resources empowers future generations to achieve their own financial goals and aspirations.

Giving Back to the Community: With financial freedom, you have the opportunity to make a positive impact on your community. Engaging in philanthropy and charitable giving allows you to support causes that are meaningful to you and contribute to the betterment of society.

The journey towards financial freedom is not solely about accumulating wealth but about creating a life of purpose, abundance, and fulfillment. As you enjoy the benefits of financial freedom, remember to remain humble and grateful for the opportunities it brings. Embrace a mindful and purpose-driven approach to life, valuing experiences, connections, and personal growth above all else. Share your success by giving back to others, supporting your loved ones, and creating a positive impact that extends far beyond yourself. Embrace the true essence of financial freedom, and let it be the catalyst for a life of abundance, contentment, and meaningful contribution.

Conclusion:

In "The Money Equation: How to Make More, Save More, and Live Richer," we have embarked on a transformative journey to unravel the secrets of financial success and empowerment. Throughout this book, we delved into the fundamental components that constitute the money equation, from cultivating the right mindset to optimizing income, managing expenses, and strategizing for the future. As we reach the conclusion of this enlightening voyage, it is imperative to reflect on the significance of the knowledge we have gained and, more importantly, the actions we must take to pave the way towards a prosperous and fulfilling financial future.

• *Emphasizing the Importance of Taking Action:*

Knowledge alone is not enough to transform one's financial situation; it is the application of that knowledge through action that generates tangible results. Understanding the principles and strategies outlined in this book is the first step on the path to financial well-being. However, without taking action, this newfound knowledge remains inert and untapped potential. As you put down this book, I implore you to take charge of your financial destiny by implementing the insights gained throughout these pages. Whether it's setting clear financial goals, creating a budget, negotiating a higher salary, or starting an investment portfolio, each step you take moves you closer to financial freedom and the life you envision.

It's natural to encounter doubts and uncertainties along the way, but remember that every successful financial journey starts with small, intentional actions.

Procrastination is the adversary of progress, and it can delay your dreams indefinitely. Therefore, I encourage you to take that first step, no matter how modest it may seem, and trust in the power of consistent effort. The path to financial freedom might not always be smooth, and setbacks may arise, but by persistently applying the principles outlined in this book, you will steadily build the foundation for a brighter financial future.

As you take action and witness the positive changes it brings, let your newfound financial empowerment inspire others around you. Share your knowledge, encourage those in your circle to embark on their own financial journeys, and create a ripple effect of financial literacy and well-being. Remember that financial success is not an isolated achievement but an opportunity to positively impact your life and the lives of those you care about.

The money equation is not an abstract concept but a dynamic tool for transforming your financial reality. Armed with the understanding and motivation gained from this book, go forth and shape your financial destiny. Take action, persevere through challenges, and seize every opportunity to enhance your financial literacy and prosperity. By doing so, you will unlock the true potential of "The Money Equation" and pave the way to make more, save more, and live richer.

- ## *Getting Started on Your Financial Journey:*

Embarking on your financial journey can feel overwhelming, but rest assured that taking the first steps is often the most challenging part. By breaking down the process into manageable actions, you can gain momentum and build a strong foundation for your financial success. Let's explore practical steps to guide you as you begin this transformative expedition towards financial empowerment.

Assess Your Current Financial Situation: To chart a course towards your financial goals, start by assessing your current financial standing. Gather all your financial documents, including bank statements, investment accounts, loans, and credit card statements. Calculate your net worth by subtracting your liabilities (debts) from your assets (savings, investments, and property). Understanding where you currently stand financially will serve as a reference point for measuring progress.

Define Your Financial Goals: Clarity of purpose is essential on any journey, and your financial expedition is no exception. Define specific, measurable, achievable, relevant, and time-bound (SMART) financial goals. Whether you aim to build an emergency fund, pay off debts, save for a down payment on a house, or retire comfortably, having clear objectives will guide your financial decisions and keep you focused.

Create a Budget: A budget is your financial roadmap, detailing how you will allocate your income to cover expenses, savings, and investments. Start by categorizing your expenses into essential (e.g., housing, food, utilities) and discretionary (e.g., entertainment, dining out). Analyze your spending patterns to identify areas where you can cut back and redirect funds toward your financial goals. Embrace the principles of frugality and disciplined spending to ensure your money aligns with your aspirations.

Build an Emergency Fund: Life is unpredictable, and having an emergency fund is like carrying a safety net wherever you go. Aim to save three to six months' worth of living expenses in a separate, easily accessible account. This fund will shield you from unexpected financial setbacks, reducing the need to rely on credit or disrupt long-term savings and investments.

Educate Yourself: Knowledge is the key that unlocks the door to financial empowerment. Educate yourself about personal finance, investment strategies, and money management. Read books, attend seminars, follow reputable financial websites, and seek guidance from financial advisors if necessary. Continuous learning will equip you with the tools to make informed decisions and adapt to changing economic landscapes.

Establish Good Financial Habits: Cultivating healthy financial habits is crucial for long-term success.

Consistency is the key to building a strong financial foundation. Set up automated savings and investment contributions to ensure you consistently allocate funds towards your goals. Prioritize debt repayment, avoid unnecessary borrowing, and pay your bills on time to maintain a positive credit history.

Embrace the Power of Compound Interest: One of the most potent tools in your financial arsenal is compound interest. Whether it's in a savings account, retirement fund, or investment portfolio, allowing your money to grow exponentially over time can significantly impact your wealth. Start investing early, even with small amounts, to leverage the power of compound interest.

Reassess and Adjust: Your financial journey is not a one-time endeavor; it's an ongoing process that requires periodic review and adjustments. Life circumstances, financial goals, and economic conditions will change, so it's essential to revisit and update your financial plan accordingly. Be flexible and open to making necessary adjustments as you progress on your journey.

Seek Support and Accountability: Sharing your financial goals with a trusted friend, family member, or financial advisor can provide valuable support and accountability. Discussing your progress and challenges with someone you trust can offer fresh perspectives and keep you motivated on your path to success.

Celebrate Milestones: Acknowledge and celebrate your financial achievements, no matter how small they may seem. Recognize the progress you make and use these milestones as encouragement to keep moving forward. Celebrating your successes will reinforce positive financial habits and remind you of the journey's significance.

Remember, your financial journey is unique to you, and it may differ from others' paths. Embrace your individuality and stay committed to your goals, making adjustments as needed. By taking these steps and staying dedicated to your financial well-being, you are poised to unlock the full potential of "The Money Equation" and achieve a future of abundance and prosperity. Happy trails on your financial journey!

• *Strategies to Stay Motivated and Focused:*

As you embark on your financial journey, staying motivated and focused is essential for maintaining the momentum required to achieve your goals. The path to financial success may present challenges and temptations, but with the right strategies, you can cultivate a resilient mindset and steer towards prosperity. Here are effective ways to keep your motivation high and stay focused on your financial objectives:

Visualize Your Financial Success: Take a moment each day to envision the financial future you desire. Imagine the freedom from debt, the comfort of a well-funded retirement, or the achievement of a significant financial goal. Visualization creates a powerful mental image of success, reinforcing your commitment to making it a reality.

Set Milestones and Celebrate Progress: Break down your long-term financial goals into smaller, achievable milestones. Celebrate each milestone you reach, regardless of its size. Recognizing your progress reinforces the positive habits you've developed and provides a sense of accomplishment, driving you forward.

Review Your Goals Regularly: Keep your financial goals visible by displaying them in a prominent place, such as on your desk or as a screensaver on your electronic devices. Regularly reviewing your objectives serves as a constant reminder of what you are working towards and helps maintain your focus.

Build a Support System: Surround yourself with like-minded individuals who share similar financial aspirations. Join online forums or local financial communities to seek advice, share experiences, and provide mutual support. Engaging with others on the same journey can provide valuable insights and encouragement during challenging times.

Stay Educated and Informed: Continue learning about personal finance, investment opportunities, and economic trends. Attend financial workshops, read books and articles, and follow reputable financial experts. Knowledge empowers you to make informed decisions, and the pursuit of knowledge keeps your mind engaged and focused.

Keep Track of Your Progress: Maintain a record of your financial journey, tracking your achievements, and assessing your setbacks. Reviewing your progress periodically helps identify patterns, areas for improvement, and keeps you accountable to your goals.

Maintain a Positive Money Mindset: Cultivate a positive and optimistic attitude towards money and financial success. Avoid dwelling on past mistakes and focus on what you can learn from them. Replace negative thoughts with affirmations that reinforce your financial goals and capabilities.

Embrace Financial Challenges as Opportunities: View financial challenges as opportunities for growth rather than insurmountable obstacles. When faced with setbacks, take them as valuable lessons and a chance to improve your financial strategies.

Limit Exposure to Negative Influences: Be mindful of negative influences that can derail your financial focus. Limit exposure to media or individuals who promote excessive spending or foster a scarcity mindset. Surround yourself with positivity and inspiration instead.

Reward Yourself Appropriately: Treat yourself occasionally when you achieve significant milestones but do so in moderation and within your budget. The occasional small indulgence can reinforce positive behavior without compromising your long-term goals.

Revisit Your "Why": Reflect on the reasons driving your financial journey. Reconnect with your core motivations regularly. Understanding the "why" behind your financial goals can provide a renewed sense of purpose during challenging times.

Remember, staying motivated and focused on your financial journey is an ongoing process that requires dedication and commitment. Embrace these strategies as tools to fortify your resolve and keep moving forward, even in the face of obstacles. As you integrate these practices into your daily life, you will find yourself well-equipped to overcome challenges, celebrate successes, and create the life of financial abundance and fulfillment you envision. By remaining steadfast in your pursuit, you will unlock the full potential of "The Money Equation" and realize a future of prosperity and well-being.

www.ingramcontent.com/pod-product-compliance
Lightning Source LLC
Chambersburg PA
CBHW072140290526
45794CB00004B/1378